Basketball

NCAA®

TRIUMPH
BOOKS
CHICAGO

Copyright © 1996 by the National Collegiate Athletic Association
All rights reserved.

The National Collegiate Athletic Association
6201 College Boulevard
Overland Park, KS 66211-2422

This cover and design treatment © Triumph Books.
Cover photo courtesy the NCAA
Typography: Sue Knopf
Referee and player icon design by Mark Anderson Design, Chicago.

This book is available at special discounts for your group or organization. For further information, contact:

Triumph Books
644 South Clark Street
Chicago, Illinois 60605
(312) 939-3330
(312) 663-3557 (fax)

Printed in Canada

User's Guide

This edition of the Official Rules of NCAA Basketball has been designed to give basketball fans of all ages a quick and easy reference guide to the action on the court.

A good place to start is in the Index (arranged by key word), where you'll find references to all the rulings on a given subject in one place.

This edition contains the following material: Official NCAA Men's and Women's Basketball Rules; and Official Basketball Rules Interpretations.

New rules or changes in the rules for 1997 are indicated by shading, as shown with this paragraph.

The Interpretations are examples of game situations that illustrate how the Rules are applied. Interpretations are indicated by a special icon, as shown in the margin of this paragraph.

Headings at the top of left-hand pages refer to the Rule under discussion; right-hand headings refer to the particular Section under discussion on that page.

Contents

User's Guide iii

Rule 1 — **Court and Equipment** 1

Rule 2 — **Officials and Their Duties** 17

Rule 3 — **Players, Substitutes and Equipment** ... 41

Rule 4 — **Definitions** 53

Rule 5 — **Scoring and Timing Regulations** 79

Rule 6 — **Live Ball and Dead Ball** 95

Rule 7 — **Out of Bounds and the Throw-in** 105

Rule 8 — **Free Throw** 115

Rule 9 — **Violations and Penalties** 121

Rule 10 — **Fouls and Penalties** 139

Official Signals 169

Index 175

Rule 1

Court and Equipment

Rule 1

Court and Equipment

Section 1 **The Game** Basketball is played by two teams of five players each. The objective is for each team to throw the ball into its own basket and to prevent the other team from scoring. The ball may be thrown, batted, rolled or dribbled in any direction, subject to restrictions laid down in the following rules.

Section 2 **The Court—Dimensions** The playing court shall be a rectangular surface free from obstructions and with dimensions of 94 feet in length and 50 feet in width. These are the dimensions for the playing court only.

Section 3 **Sidelines, End Lines, Restraining Line**
a. The playing court shall be marked with sidelines, end lines and other lines as shown on the court diagram on page 4. There shall be at least 3 feet (and preferably 10 feet) of unobstructed space outside. It is legal to use contrasting colored floor areas instead of the 2-inch lines.
b. There shall be a 2-inch wide, broken restraining line, consisting of 12-inch segments, 12 inches apart, of a color different from the boundary, at a minimum of 6 feet outside the court, extending from sideline to sideline and parallel to the end line. Nonplaying personnel are not permitted in this area.

Section 4 **Center Circle** A 2-inch-wide restraining circle shall be drawn in the center of the court and shall have a radius of 6 feet measured to the outside. Spaces for nonjumpers around the restraining circle are 36 inches deep.

Court and Equipment

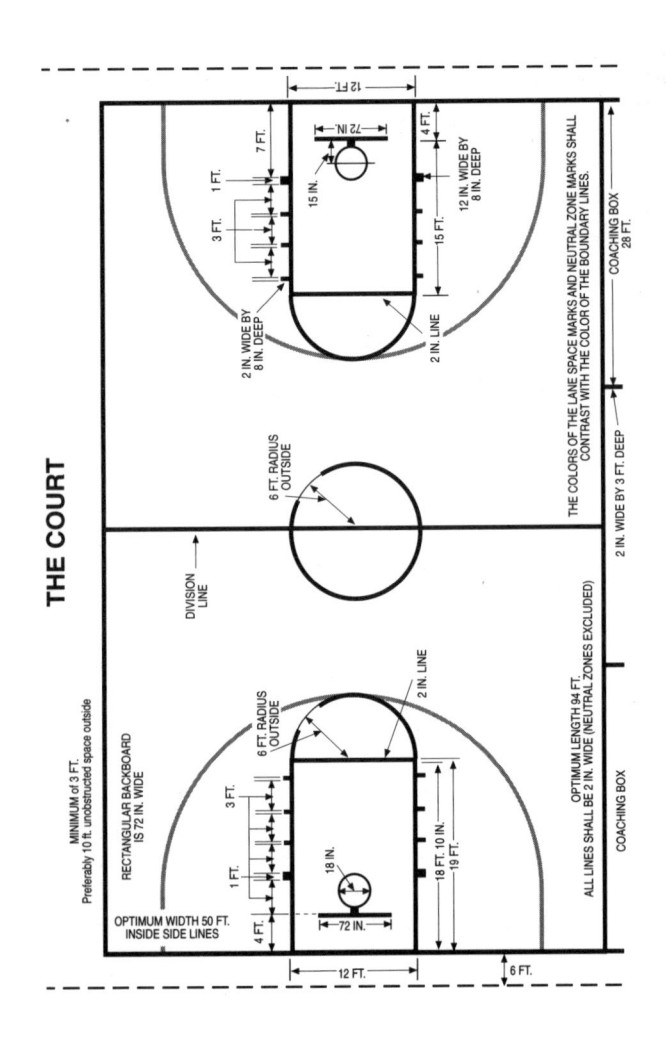

THE COURT

Court and Equipment

THE THREE-POINT FIELD-GOAL LINE

Official Rules

Notes to Court Diagram

1. If possible, building plans should provide for a court with ideal measurements as stated in Rule 1-2, ample out-of-bounds area and needed seating space. A long court permits use of two crosswise courts for practice and informal games.

2. The ceiling should be at least 25 feet and higher if possible.

3. Instead of the 2-inch boundaries mentioned in Rules 1-3, 1-4 and 1-6, it is legal to use contrasting colored floor areas by painting the out-of-bounds area, the center circle and the restricted parts of the free-throw lanes so that the mathematical line between the two colors is the boundary. If such a contrasting colored out-of-bounds belt is used, it should be at least 8 inches wide.

4. The committee recommends that a belt 8 inches or more in width be used to mark the boundaries on all courts that have at least 10 feet of open space between the boundary lines and the seating. This plan is urged for all new construction and for other similar courts when the boundaries are remarked.

5. The court should be uniformly and adequately lighted. Lighting engineers should be placed in charge of this important factor when planning any new installations. For information on recommended specifications for lighting, contact the Illuminating Engineering Society of North America, 120 Wall Street, 17th Floor, New York, New York 10005; telephone 212/248-5000.

6. See Rule 1-16 for specifications on size and placement of commercial logos.

Section 5   **Division Line**   A division line 2 inches wide dividing the court into two parts shall be formed by extending the center-circle diameter in both directions until it intersects the sidelines.

Section 6   **Free-Throw Lane**   A free-throw lane, 12 feet wide measured to the outside of each lane boundary and the semicircle with the free-throw line as a diameter, shall be marked at each end of the court with dimensions and markings as shown on the court diagram. All lines designating the free-throw lane, but not lane-space marks and neutral-zone marks, are part of the lane. The color of the lane-space marks and neutral-zone marks shall contrast with the color of the lane boundary lines. The lane-space marks (2 inches by 8 inches) and neutral-zone marks (12 inches by 8 inches) identify areas that extend from the outer edge of the lane lines 36 inches toward the sidelines. There are four marked lane spaces on each lane line.

Section 7   **Free-Throw Line**   A free-throw line, 2 inches wide, shall be drawn across each of the semicircles that have an outside radius of 6 feet as shown on the court diagram. The free-throw line shall be parallel to the end line and shall have its farther edge 15 feet from the plane of the face of the backboard.

Section 8   **Backboards—Dimensions, Material**   A transparent, rigid, rectangular backboard with a flat surface shall be used (backboards shall not be tinted). The backboards shall be similar in size at both ends of the court. The size of the backboard may be either of two dimensions: a. 6 feet horizontally and 3½ feet vertically; or b. 6 feet horizontally and 4 feet vertically as shown on the diagrams. The 6 feet horizontal and 3½ feet vertical

Court and Equipment

dimensions are recommended for replacement backboards or new installations.

It shall be marked as follows: A rectangle shall be centered behind the ring and marked by a 2-inch white line. The rectangle shall have outside dimensions of 24 inches horizontally and 18 inches vertically. The top edge of the base line shall be level with the ring.

The border on the backboard shall be 2 inches minimum and 3 inches maximum from the outside edge of the backboard.

No protrusions below the backboard shall be allowed. *Note: Any backboard support, all of which is not directly behind the backboard, should be at least 6 inches behind it if the support extends above the top and at least 2 feet behind it if the support extends beyond the side.*

Section 9 **Backboards—Padding** The bottom and each side of the all-rectangular backboards shall be padded with a Poly High-Car vinyl type material that meets the Bashor resilience test with a range of 20-30. The padding must cover the bottom surface of the board and the side surface to a distance of 15 inches up from the bottom. The front and back surface must be covered to a minimum distance of three-fourths inch from the bottom of the backboard. The padding shall be 1 inch thick from the front and back surfaces of the backboard. The material shall be 2 inches from the bottom edge of the backboard. It is recommended that the padding be mounted on the backboard by adhesive or material such as velcro, channel, etc. The padding shall be a single solid color and shall be the same color on both backboards. When it becomes necessary to use a substitute backboard, the padding shall be of the same color as the backboard being replaced.

Backboards—Positions

Section 10 **Backboards—Support Systems**

a. Padding—Any backboard support behind the backboard and at a height of less than 9 feet above the floor shall be padded on the bottom surface to a distance of 2 feet from the face of the backboard. All portable backstops must have the bases padded to a height of 7 feet on the court-side surface.

b. Clearances—As below and behind backboards, all support systems should be at least 8 feet behind the plane of the backboard face and at a height of 7 feet or more above the floor.

c. Warning on misuse of portable backstops—Manufacturers and administrators should be aware of an "extreme-caution" warning relative to the misuse of portable backstops. A high degree of injury potential and a severe liability problem exists when players or spectators are allowed to hang, sit or stand on the basket ring or backboard. Administrators must see that this practice is eliminated or that the portable units are lowered at the completion of the game. There is a high risk of severe injury, even death, if this practice continues. A recommended warning or inscription such as "Danger—please do not get on the rim/backboard" is desirable.

Section 11 **Backboards—Positions** The backboard shall be midway between the sidelines, with the plane of its front face perpendicular to the floor, parallel to the end line and 4 feet from it. The upper edge of the backboard shall be 13 feet above the floor. The backboards shall be protected from spectators to a distance of at least 3 feet at each end. Portable backboards shall be secured to the floor so as to prevent movement.

It is recommended that a locking device/safety arrester be used for ceiling and wall-mount backboard systems that are retracted by motor-pulley cable arrangements.

Court and Equipment

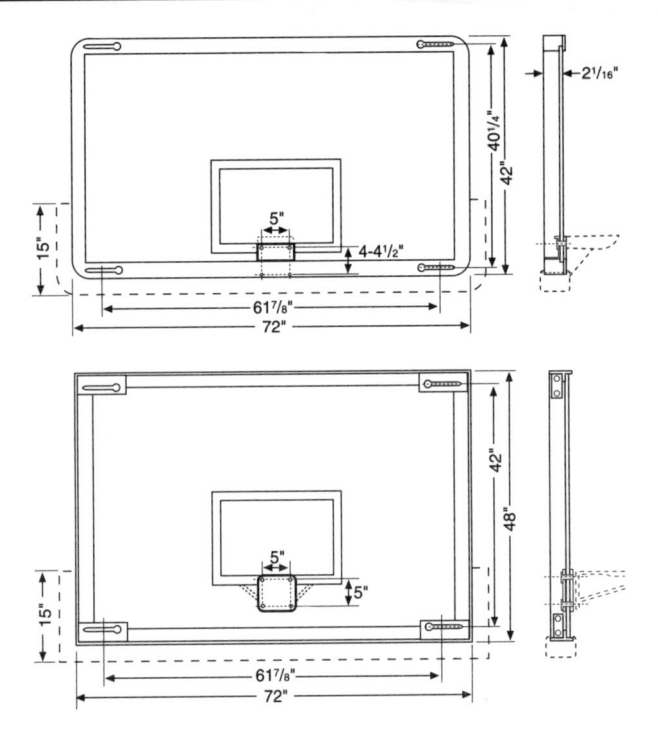

Section 12 **Baskets—Size, Material** Each basket shall consist of a single metal ring, 18 inches in inside diameter, its flange and braces, and a white-cord, 12-mesh net, 15 to 18 inches in length, suspended from beneath the ring. Each ring shall be not more than five-eighths of an inch in diameter, with the possible addition of small-gauge loops on the under-edge for attaching a 12-mesh net. The ring and its attaching flange and braces shall be bright orange in color. The cord of the net shall be not less than 120-thread nor more than 144-thread twine, or plastic material of comparable dimensions

and constructed so as to check the ball momentarily as it passes through.

Section 13   **Baskets—Position** Each basket ring shall be securely attached to the backboard/support system with a rim-restraining device. Such a device will ensure that the basket stays attached, even in the event that a glass backboard breaks. Each basket ring shall have its upper edge 10 feet above and parallel to the floor and shall be equidistant from the vertical edges of the backboard. The nearest point of the inside edge of the ring shall be 6 inches from the plane of the face of the backboard.

Movable and nonmovable rings are legal. A movable basket ring shall have rebound characteristics identical to those of a nonmovable ring. The pressure-release mechanism should ensure these characteristics, as well as protect both the ring and backboard. The design of the ring and its construction should be such as to ensure player safety.

It is recommended that all competitive rings be tested three times during the season for rebound/elasticity to ensure that this component is maintained. This should be done with a nonmechanical, tamper-proof, computational testing device that determines the amount of energy absorption as a calibration. The rebound/elasticity of any basket ring support system shall be within a 35 percent to 50 percent energy absorption range of total impact energy and within a five percent differential between baskets on the same court.

The pressure-release/elasticity mechanism on movable rings may be field adjustable. When released, the ring shall not rotate more than 30 degrees below the original horizontal position. After release and with the load no longer applied, the ring shall return automatically and instantaneously to the original position.

Court and Equipment

> It is recommended that basket ring loads be transferred to the support system by a single strut boom behind the backboard or to the backboard frame.

Section 14 **The Ball—Specifications, Color** The ball shall be spherical. Its color shall be the approved orange shade. It shall have a deeply pebbled leather cover unless both teams agree to use a ball with a nonleather cover. The ball shall have the traditionally shaped eight panels, bonded tightly to the rubber carcass. Only the manufacturer's name and/or logo is permitted on the basketball.

a. (Men) The width of the black rubber rib (channels and/or seams) shall not exceed one-fourth inch. The circumference of the ball shall be within a maximum of 30 inches and a minimum of 29½ inches. Its weight shall not be less than 20 ounces nor more than 22 ounces.

b. (Women) The width of the black rubber rib (channels and/or seams) shall not exceed one-fourth inch. The circumference of the ball shall be within a maximum of 29 inches and a minimum of 28½ inches. Its weight shall not be less than 18 ounces nor more than 20 ounces.

The ball shall be inflated to an air pressure such that when it is dropped to the playing surface from a height of 6 feet measured to the bottom of the ball, it will rebound to a height, measured to the top of the ball;

c. (Men) of not less than 49 inches when it strikes on its least resilient spot nor more than 54 inches when it strikes on its most resilient spot.

d. (Women) of not less than 51 inches when it strikes on its least resilient spot nor more than 56 inches when it strikes on its most resilient spot.

When dribbled vertically, without rotation, the ball shall return directly to the dribbler's hand.

Note: The air pressure that will give the required reaction must be stamped on the ball in order for it to be legal. The pressure for game use must be such as to make the ball bounce legally.

Section 15   **New Equipment**   The NCAA Men's and Women's Basketball Rules Committees are responsible for formulating the official playing rules for the sport. The committees are not responsible for testing or approving playing equipment for use in intercollegiate men's and women's basketball.

Equipment manufacturers have undertaken the responsibility for the development of playing equipment that meets the size and weight specifications established from time to time by the committees. The NCAA urges manufacturers to work with the various independent testing agencies to ensure the production of safe products. Neither the NCAA nor the NCAA Men's and Women's Basketball Rules Committees certify the safety of any basketball equipment. Only equipment that meets the weight and size dimensions specified in the NCAA Men's and Women's Basketball Rules may be used in intercollegiate competition.

While the committees do not regulate the development of new equipment and do not set technical or scientific standards for testing equipment or the approval or disapproval of specific playing equipment, the committees may, from time to time, provide manufacturers with informal guidelines as to the equipment-performance levels they consider consistent with the integrity of the game. The committees reserve the right to intercede in order to protect and maintain that integrity.

The NCAA Men's and Women's Basketball Rules Committees suggest that manufacturers planning innovative changes in basketball equipment submit the equipment to the NCAA Men's and Women's Basketball Rules Committees for review before production.

Court and Equipment

SECTION 16 **Logos/Names** Logos and/or names of any kind (including school and conference logos or names) are not permitted on the backboard, rims and padding around the backboard or on or attached to the shot clock. Only the manufacturer's name and/or logo is permitted on the basketball. Commercial logos are permitted on the playing court but must conform to the following standards: The logo must fit into a box that is 10 feet by 10 feet square; the logo must be located 8½ feet from the mid-court division line and 4½ feet from the sideline; logos are limited to not more than two exposures, with no more than one in each half of the court.

Section 17 **Ball—Provided by Home Team** The home team shall provide a ball that meets the specifications of Rule 1-14. The referee shall be the sole judge of the legality of the ball and may select for use a ball provided by the visiting team if the home team cannot provide a legal ball.

INTERPRETATION

Play: Visiting Team B's captain notices that Team B's pre-game warm-up balls are of a different type than the official game ball. Team B's coach requests that Team B be allowed to warm up using the type of ball being used in the game.

Ruling: Official shall inform the home Team A's game management that Team B must be allowed to warm up with the same type of ball(s) that will be used during the game.

Section 18 **Scoreboard, Game-Clock Display** A visible game clock and scoreboard are mandatory. It is permissible to place a red warning light behind each backboard to indicate that the period-ending horn has sounded. An alternate timing device and scoring display must be available in the event of malfunctions.

Section 19 **Shot-Clock Displays** The shot clocks shall be recessed on top of each backboard. If it is not possible to recess the clocks, they shall be mounted on the wall and positioned to the left of each basket as viewed from the center of the court. If it is not possible to recess or mount the clocks on the wall, they shall, as a last resort, be located on the floor at each end of the court so that they are visible to players and the shot-clock operator.

A visible shot clock is mandatory. An alternate timing device must be available in the event the visible shot clock malfunctions.

Section 20 **Possession Indicator** A visible display must be available to indicate team possession in the alternating-possession process.

Section 21 **Team Benches—Scorers' and Timers' Table** The team benches shall be located equidistant from the division line extended at each side of the scorers' and timers' table on the sidelines.

Choice of benches is made by the home-team game administration.

Teams shall warm up and shoot at the end of the court farthest from their own bench for the first half.

Section 22 **Coaching Box** A coaching box shall be outlined outside the side of the court on which the scorers'/timers' table and team benches are located. The area shall be bounded by the end line extended, sideline, a line 28 feet from the end line, and the team bench. The end line and 28-foot lines shall be 3 feet long and 2 inches

Court and Equipment

wide and shall contrast in color with that of the sideline and end line. If the team bench starts less than 28 feet from the end line and extends beyond the end line, the coaching box shall extend from one end of the bench to the other.

Section 23 **Three-Point Field-Goal Line** A three-point field-goal line, in the form of a semicircle 2 inches wide, shall be drawn at each end of the court. The semicircle has a radius of 19 feet 9 inches from the center of the basket to the outside of the line. The semicircle line shall be extended with a 2-inch-wide line perpendicular to the end line whose length shall be 63 inches from the inside edge of the end line. The three-point field-goal line shall be the same color as the free-throw lane boundary lines.

Rule 2

Officials and Their Duties

Rule 2

Officials and Their Duties

Section 1 **The Officials** The officials shall be:
a. A referee and an umpire, or
b. A referee and two umpires, who shall be assisted by two timers, two scorers and a shot-clock operator. A single timer and single scorer may be used if they are trained personnel acceptable to the referee. The scorers, timers and operator shall be located at the scorers' and timers' table on the side of the court.

The officials shall conduct the game in accordance with the official rules and interpretations and employ the mechanics of officiating outlined in an NCAA-approved basketball officials manual. This includes notifying the captain when play is about to begin at the start of the game, after an intermission or charged timeout, or after any unusual delay in putting the ball in play; determining when the ball becomes dead; prohibiting practice during a dead ball, except between halves; administering penalties; ordering and assessing timeouts; beckoning substitutes to enter the court; indicating a successful three-point field goal by raising two arms overhead; and silently and visibly counting seconds to administer Rules 7-5, 7-6, 8-3, 9-1-b-(1) and 9-9. No official has the authority to set aside any official rules or approved interpretations.
Note: The officials' uniform shall be a black-and-white striped shirt and black pants.

Section 2 **The Referee—Duties** The referee shall inspect and approve all equipment, including court, baskets, ball,

Officials and Their Duties

backboards and timers' and scorers' signals. Before the scheduled starting time of the game, the referee shall designate the official timepieces, operators, the official scorebook and official scorer. The referee shall be responsible for seeing that each team is notified three minutes before each half is to begin. The referee shall toss the ball at center to start the first and extra periods; decide whether a goal will count if the officials disagree; have the power to forfeit a game when conditions warrant; and decide matters upon which the timers and scorers disagree.

Section 3 **Approval of Score** At the end of each half, the referee shall check and approve the score. The referee's approval at the end of the game terminates the jurisdiction of the officials. When the referee leaves the playing court at the end of the game, the referee's jurisdiction has ended and the score has been approved.

INTERPRETATIONS

Play 1: (Men) Team A is ahead by one point. The game-ending horn sounds with the ball at mid-court. Player A1 grabs the ball and dunks the ball in the basket and hangs on the basket clearly after playing time has expired. Referee, who is at the foul line and on the way to the scorers' table to approve the final score, sees this action by A1 and assesses two technical fouls. Coach of Team A pushes the referee after the technical fouls have been called. Official banishes the coach from the game and awards six free throws in total to Team B.
Ruling: Official is correct. Officials' jurisdiction is still in effect because referee had not approved the final score. Official may call a technical foul, an official's correctable error (Rule 2-10), or scorer's bookkeeping

Unsporting Conduct

error up until the referee has approved the final score.

Play 2: Officials leave the playing court and while they are in the locker room, it is discovered that there is a mistake in the score or there was a request for a legal correctable error (Rule 2-10) by the losing coach when the game ended.
Ruling: Once the officials leave the playing court at the end of the game, their jurisdiction has ended, and the score has been approved.

Section 4   **Elastic Power**   The referee shall have power to make decisions on any points not specifically covered in the rules.

Section 5   **Television Monitors**   Replay equipment or television monitoring may be used only in situations involved in preventing or rectifying a scorer's or timer's mistake or malfunctioning game or shot clocks and to determine if a fight occurred and those individuals who participated in a fight. Officials may not use replay equipment for judgment calls such as who fouled, basket interference or goaltending, release of the ball before the sounding of the horn, etc.

Section 6   **Unsporting Conduct**   The officials shall penalize unsporting conduct by any player, coach, substitute, team attendant or follower. If there is flagrant misconduct, the officials shall penalize by removing any offending player from the game and banishing any offending coach, substitute, team attendant or follower to the locker room. A player who commits a fifth foul, including any combination of personal, unsporting and contact technical fouls, shall be removed from the game. The official will notify the coach and player of a disqualification.

Officials and Their Duties

INTERPRETATIONS

Play 1: A1 who has been disqualified: (a) reports to the scorer and is subsequently beckoned onto the court by the official; or (b) after reporting to the scorer and being beckoned onto the court, is not discovered until he or she has participated and scored.

Ruling: Flagrant technical foul in both (a) and (b). A1 is removed from the game immediately upon discovery and the offended team is awarded two free throws and given the ball out of bounds at the center of the court for a throw-in. In (b), any score made by A1 is counted (Rule 10-2).

Play 2: Who is responsible for behavior of spectators?
Ruling: The home management or game committee, insofar as they reasonably can be expected to control the spectators. The officials may call fouls on either team if its supporters act in such a way as to interfere with the proper conduct of the game. Discretion must be used in calling such fouls, however, lest a team be unjustly penalized.

Section 7 **When Officials' Decisions Differ** No official shall have authority to set aside or question decisions made by the other(s) within the limits of their respective outlined duties. The referee's decision does not take precedence over an umpire(s) in calling a foul or violation.

INTERPRETATION

Play: The umpire observes traveling, or stepping out of bounds or another violation by A1. At approximately the same time, A1 tries for a field goal or the referee observes contact by B1.

Ruling: The officials must decide which act occurred first. There is nothing inherent in such acts to make it necessary to rule them as occurring simultaneously. If the violation occurred first, the ball became dead. If the ball was in flight during the try before the traveling or the touching of the boundary, there was no violation. If the contact occurred after a violation was observed, it was not a foul unless an unsporting factor was involved.

Section 8   **Time and Place of Jurisdiction**   The officials shall have power to make decisions for infractions of rules committed either within or outside the boundary lines from 30 minutes for men and 15 minutes for women before the scheduled starting time of the game through the referee's approval of the final score. This includes the periods when the game may be momentarily stopped for any reason. For men, at least one official shall arrive on the floor 30 minutes before the start of the game. When the referee leaves the playing court at the end of the game, the referee's jurisdiction has ended and the score has been approved.

INTERPRETATION

Play: At approximately 12 minutes before the time the game is scheduled to start, the referee asks the scorekeeper whether the teams have submitted their squad lists and their starting lineups. The referee is told that Team A has not.

Ruling: The referee may, but is not obligated to, suggest to the scorer that the scorer remind the coach of Team A that the submission of the squad list and starting lineup is required at least 10 minutes before the assigned time of the game.

Section 9   **Signals for Fouls and Throw-ins**
a. When a foul occurs, an official shall signal the timer to stop the clock, designate the offender to the scorers and indicate with fingers the number of free throws.

Note: It is strongly recommended that a player charged with a foul raise only one hand at arm's length above the head and lower it in such a manner as not to indicate resentment.

b. When a team is entitled to a throw-in, an official shall clearly signal the act that caused the ball to become dead, the throw-in spot unless it follows a successful goal or an awarded goal, and the team entitled to the throw-in. The official shall hand (not toss) the ball to or place the ball at the disposal of the thrower-in for a throw-in unless the throw-in is from outside an end line after a successful goal.

INTERPRETATION

Play: Team B has scored a field goal, and A1 has the ball along the end line for a throw-in. Team A is not in the bonus. Before the ball is thrown inbounds by A1: (a) B1 fouls A2 inbounds near A1; or (b) B1 fouls A2 at the division line; or (c) B1 fouls A2 beyond the division line.

Ruling: In (a), (b) and (c), the ball is awarded out of bounds at the spot closest to where the foul occurred. Team A may not run the end line, due to the fact that when a foul is called, it negates the right to run the end line after a score. The calling of a timeout does not negate the right to run the end line.

Section 10 **Correctable Errors** Officials may correct an error if a rule inadvertently is set aside and results in the following:
 a. Failure to award a merited free throw.
 b. Awarding an unmerited free throw.
 c. Permitting a wrong player to attempt a free throw.
 d. Attempting a free throw at the wrong basket.
 e. Erroneously counting or canceling a score.
 In order to correct any of the five officials' errors (a-e) listed above, such error must be recognized by an

official before the first dead ball becomes live after the clock has started. If an official's error (e) is made while the clock is running and the ball is dead, it must be recognized before the second live ball after the error.

When correcting officials' errors (a) and (b), the officials shall (1) award only the merited free throws that have not been attempted or (2) nullify only the successful unmerited free throws.

If the error is a free throw by the wrong player (c) or at the wrong basket (d) or the awarding of an unmerited free throw (b), the free throw and the activity during it, other than unsporting conduct, flagrant, intentional or technical fouls, shall be canceled. However, other points scored, consumed time and additional activity, which may occur before the recognition of a mistake, shall not be nullified. Errors because of free-throw attempts by the wrong player or at the wrong basket shall be corrected by applying Rules 8-1 and 8-2.

If an error is corrected, play shall be resumed from the point at which it was interrupted to correct the error.

INTERPRETATIONS

Play 1: B1 pushes A1 during a try and the try is not successful. A1 is awarded two free throws. The first free throw by A1 is successful, after which B2 completes a throw-in to B3, who passes to B4 for an easy lay-up at the basket of Team B. The captain of Team A then calls attention to the referee that A1 did not receive a second free throw.
Ruling The goal by B4 counts. The referee shall permit A1 to attempt the second free throw with no players lined up along the free-throw lane. The ball is then awarded to Team A out of bounds at the end line by Team B's basket, which was the point of interruption to correct the error.

Play 2: After the bonus provision is in effect, B1 holds A1. Erroneously A1 is not awarded a bonus opportunity. A1 is awarded the ball out of bounds and completes a throw-in to A2. The coach of Team A notifies the scorer that the coach wants to meet with the official concerning a correctable error. When A scores a field goal, the scorer sounds the horn and advises the official of the coach's request for the conference. The official recognizes the correctable error after talking with the coach.
Ruling: The goal by A counts and this error is correctable because it is within the prescribed time limitation of Rule 2-10. When a correctable error is called to the scorer's attention by a coach while the clock is running, the scorer will not use the sounding device until the ball has become dead.

Play 3: Before the bonus rule goes into effect, B1 blocks A1. The official errs by awarding A1 a one-and-one attempt. (a) A1 makes the first free-throw try, and the error is then discovered; or (b) A1 is successful in both free-throw attempts, and then the official detects the error; or (c) A1 misses the first of the one-and-one attempts and the clock starts, at which time the official detects the error; or (d) A1 is successful in the first bonus attempt but misses the second free-throw try and, as a result, the clock starts and B1 advances to score. In each of the four situations, it was called to the attention of the official before the first dead ball became live after the clock had started.
Ruling: In each of the four situations, the error is correctable. In (a), (b), and (c), Team A is awarded the ball at the spot out of bounds nearest to where the foul occurred. In (d), Team A is awarded the ball out of bounds at Team B's end line, which was the point of interruption to rectify the error. Any free throws that were made in any of the four situations are canceled.

Correctable Errors

Play 4: B1 holds A1 after the bonus provision is in effect. Inadvertently A1 is not awarded the bonus opportunity. Team A is awarded the ball out of bounds, and A1 receives the throw-in. Team A controls the ball in-bounds, and A3 eventually asks for and receives a timeout. During the timeout, the referee either recognizes the referee's own error or it is called to his or her attention that A1 should have been awarded a one-and-one free throw opportunity.
Ruling: A1 is awarded the one-and-one with no players lining up along the free-throw lane and play is resumed at the point of interruption, which is the spot out of bounds nearest to where the ball was when time-out was granted.

Play 5: B1 fouls A1, and Team A is not in the bonus. The official erroneously awards A1 a one-and-one. After the second free throw is successful, the captain of Team B calls the error to the official's attention.
Ruling: The official recognizes the error. The official shall cancel both free throws and award the ball to Team A at the out-of-bounds spot nearest to where the foul by B1 occurred.

Play 6: B1 fouls A1, and Team A is not in the bonus. The official erroneously awards A1 a one-and-one. A1 is successful on the first try; however, the second is missed and B1 rebounds the ball. B1 dribbles down the floor and scores a field goal. The official is called to the bench by the coach of Team B who points out that A1 erroneously had been awarded a one-and-one.
Ruling: The official orders the scorer to cancel A1's successful free throw. The ball is then awarded to Team A for a throw-in and is taken to the end line by B's basket, which was the point of interruption.

Officials and Their Duties

Play 7: B1 fouls A1 and it is Team B's 10th foul of the first half. The official erroneously awards A1 a one-and-one. The first free throw is unsuccessful and B1 rebounds the ball and requests a timeout. During the timeout, the official is notified that A1 should have been awarded two free throws instead of a one-and-one.
Ruling: As A1 has already attempted one free throw, A1 is permitted to attempt a second free throw with no players lined up along the free-throw lane. The ball is then awarded to Team B out of bounds for a throw-in after the timeout.

Play 8: B1 fouls A1 and it is Team B's ninth foul of the second half. The official erroneously awards A1 two free throws instead of a one-and-one. A1 (a) successfully completes two free throws, or (b) misses the first free-throw attempt and successfully completes the second free-throw attempt, or (c) misses both free-throw attempts. Within the correctable error time limitations, the officials are notified of their error.
Ruling: In (a), A1 was entitled to the second free-throw attempt because the first free throw was successful. Both free throws count, and play is resumed at the point of interruption. In (b), A1's first free throw, to which he or she was entitled as the first part of a one-and-one, was unsuccessful, and the player should not have been awarded a second free-throw attempt. The successful second free-throw attempt is nullified, and play is resumed at the point of interruption. In (c), A1's unmerited second free-throw attempt was unsuccessful so it is ignored, and play is resumed at the point of interruption.

Play 9: (a) A1, or (b) B1 is called for basket interference at basket of Team A. In (a), the referee erroneously counts score or, in (b), erroneously fails to count it. In each case, the error is discovered before the first dead

ball has become live after the clock has started.
Ruling: The official's error in both (a) and (b) is correctable because the error was recognized within the proper time limit.

Play 10: A1 is fouled by B1 during a field-goal attempt and the try is successful. A2 erroneously is awarded the free throw. While A2's successful attempt is in the air: (a) B1 fouls A3, or (b) B1 intentionally fouls A3. Before the ball becomes live, the coach of Team B properly asks the referee to correct the error of awarding the free throw to the wrong player.
Ruling: The free throw by A2 is canceled; and A1 will properly attempt the free throw. The common foul by B1 in (a) is canceled. The intentional foul in (b) cannot be canceled. The error is corrected when A1 is given the free-throw attempt, which A1 was entitled to as a result of the original foul. In (b), the game continues with the administration of the two free throws to A3 resulting from the intentional foul by B1. Team A is awarded the ball out of bounds at the spot nearest to where the foul occurred.

Play 11: Team B has (a) six players participating simultaneously; or (b) a player who has changed his or her number and failed to report the change to the scorer and an official; or (c) a player who has been disqualified for committing five personal fouls or a flagrant foul; or (d) squad members of the same team wearing identical numbers.
Ruling: In (a), Team B is assessed a technical foul. In (d), each offender is assessed a technical foul. In (b) and (c), each offender is assessed a flagrant technical foul. Each of these infractions is penalized any time it is discovered while the rule is being violated. In (b) and (c), the player is disqualified and must go to the locker room

Play 12: A5 is fouled during an unsuccessful try for goal. As A5 goes to the foul line, A5 is assessed an unsporting technical foul, which is A5's fifth and disqualifying foul. The scorer (a) informs the official that A5 has been disqualified, or (b) does not inform the official that A5 has been disqualified and A5 attempts the free throws.

Ruling: In (a), the official informs A5 and the coach that A5 is disqualified and the substitute must attempt the free throws. In (b), if A5 makes either or both or none of the free throws and the error is discovered within the time limitations of the correctable error rule, any successful free throw(s) is canceled and A5's substitute must attempt the free throw(s). After the free throws are attempted, the ball is put in play at the point of interruption to correct the error.

Play 13: Defensive player B1 commits a fifth foul (any combination of personal, unsporting and contact technical fouls), which results in two free throws for A1. The official scorer and timer fail to notify either of the game officials or the player (B1) that a fifth foul has been committed. When the scorers realize the error, they inform the timer to sound the sounding device. The timer sounds the device as the first free-throw attempt is made or missed. The referee then asks the table personnel to explain the problem. The official is advised that B1 has committed five fouls, upon which the referee then advises the coach and player of Team B that B1 has five fouls. The coach then replaces B1. Is any free throw awarded to Team A?

Ruling: No. This is an inadvertent error for which B1 is not responsible; no penalty is applied.

Play 14: With Team A leading 51 to 50, a held ball is called. A6 properly reports and enters the game. Time is then called by Team A. The timepiece shows three

Duties of Scorers

seconds remaining in the game. After play is resumed by a throw-in, the official: (a) recognizes that Team A has six players competing; or (b) does not notice Team A has six players on the court. Time then expires, and Team B now reports to the officials that Team A had six players on the court. In each case, the officials could not get the clock stopped before time expired for the end of the game.

Ruling: In (a), one of the officials had knowledge Team A had six players participating simultaneously and thus the error was detected before time expired; therefore, a technical foul would be assessed against A6. In (b), the error was not called to the official's attention until after time had expired and it was too late to assess any penalty.

Play 15: The game is in the first overtime period. It is discovered that: (a) A1 took an excess timeout during the second half; or (b) A6 was playing without having reported to the scorer; or (c) A2, who is in the game, changed his or her shirt number without reporting the change.

Ruling: In (a) and (b), the errors are ignored unless discovered before the ball becomes live since they do not come under the correctable-error rule (Rule 2-10). In (c), disqualify A2 and award two free throws to Team B.

Section 11 — **Duties of Scorers** The scorers shall record the field goals made and the free throws made and missed and shall keep a running summary of the points scored. They shall record the personal and technical fouls called on each player and shall notify an official immediately when the fifth foul, including any combination of personal, unsporting and contact technical fouls, or the third noncontact technical foul is called on a squad member or bench personnel. They shall notify an official immediately when a second technical foul for unsporting conduct is charged directly to a coach, squad member or any bench personnel. They shall record anyone who has been ejected for fighting as determined by the referee. They shall record the timeouts charged to each team and shall notify a team and its head coach, through an official, whenever that team takes its final allowable charged timeout. They shall signal the nearer official each time a team is granted a charged timeout in excess of the legal number and in each half when a player commits a common foul beginning with the team's seventh foul and for men, the team's 10th foul, including any combination of personal, unsporting and contact technical fouls.

The score book of the home team shall be the official book, unless the referee rules otherwise. The official score book shall remain at the scorers' table throughout the game including all intermissions. The scorers shall compare their records after each goal, each foul and each charged timeout, notifying the referee at once of any discrepancy. If the error cannot be found, the referee shall accept the record of the official book, unless the referee has knowledge that permits another decision. If the discrepancy is in the score and the error is not resolved, the referee shall accept the progressive team totals of the official score book. A scoring or bookkeeping error may be corrected at any time until the referee has approved the score at the end of the game.

The scorers shall keep a record of the names and numbers of players who are to start the game and of all substitutes who enter the game. It is recommended that squad members' names be entered in the score book in numerical order. When there is an infraction of the rules pertaining to submission of the roster, substitutions or numbers of players, they shall notify the nearer official.

Duties of Scorers

To signal the officials, the scorers shall use a sounding device unlike that used by the referee and umpire. This may be used immediately if (or as soon as) the ball is dead or is in control of the offending team.

Note: It is recommended that only the official scorer wear a black-and-white-striped garment, and the official scorer's location shall be clearly marked. It is recommended that an "X," 12 inches long and 2 inches wide, be placed on the floor out of bounds and directly in front of the scorer for ease in identifying the scorer.

INTERPRETATIONS

Play 1: At half time, the official scorer, who is a member of the home-team faculty, removes the scorebook from the table: (a) of his or her own volition; or (b) at the request of the home-team coach.

Ruling: In (a), if the removal is inadvertent and momentary, there would be no penalty. If there is evidence that the scorer removed the scorebook to take it to the home-team dressing room, a foul could be assessed if the official had directed the official scorer not to do so. In (b), if the home-team coach requests the official scorer to remove the book, and this is done after the official had directed the scorer not to do so, the home team would be assessed a technical foul.

Play 2: The scorer fails to record two points awarded to Team A by the official during the first half as a result of basket interference by B2.

Ruling: The score should be corrected.

Play 3: After two minutes of the first overtime period have been played, it is discovered that during the second half of regulation play the scorer failed to record one point as a result of a free throw by Team A.

Officials and Their Duties

Ruling: The score should be corrected and play should be continued.

Play 4: A player who has committed a fifth foul (any combination of personal, unsporting and contact technical fouls) continues to play because the scorers have failed to notify the officials.

Ruling: As soon as the scorers discover the irregularity, they should sound the horn after (or as soon as) the ball is in control of the offending team or is dead. The disqualified player must be removed immediately. Any points that may have been scored while such player was illegally in the game are counted. If other aspects of the error are correctable, the procedure to be followed is included among the duties of officials (Rule 2-10).

Play 5: The scorer's horn sounds while the ball is live.
Ruling: Players should ignore the horn since it does not make the ball dead. The officials must use their judgment in blowing the ball dead to consult the scorers.

Play 6: The scorers fail to notify a team or its coach when it takes its final allowable charged timeout.
Ruling: The team should be penalized with a technical foul if it requests an excessive timeout.

Section 12 **Duties of Timers** The timers shall note when each half is to start and shall notify the referee more than three minutes before the half is to start. They shall signal the scorers three minutes before starting time. They shall record playing time and time of stoppages, as provided in the rules.

The timers shall be provided with a game clock to be used for timing periods and intermissions and a stopwatch for timing timeouts. The game clock shall be operated by one of the timers. The game clock and stopwatch shall be placed so that they may be seen by both timers.

Duties of Timers

The clock shall be started as prescribed in Rule 5-12.

Fifteen seconds before the expiration of an intermission or a charged timeout, the timer shall sound a warning signal. A second signal shall be given at the expiration of the timeout. Timeouts are 75 seconds in games that do not have a media timeout format. Play shall be resumed immediately upon the sounding of the second signal.

The game clock shall be stopped at the expiration of time for each period and when an official signals timeout, as in Rule 5-10. The game clock also shall be stopped after successful field goals in the last minute of the game and the last minute of any overtime period with no substitution allowed during the dead-ball situation. For a charged timeout, the timers shall start the stopwatch and shall signal the referee when it is time to resume play. Ten seconds before the expiration of the 30-second time limit to replace a disqualified player a warning signal shall be sounded. The signal also shall be sounded at the end of 30 seconds to replace a disqualified player.

Expiration of playing time in each half or extra period shall be indicated by the timers' signal. This signal terminates player activity. If the timers' signal fails to sound, or is not heard, the timers shall go on the court or use other means to notify the referee immediately. If, in the meantime, a goal has been made or a foul has occurred, the referee shall consult the timers. If the timers agree that time expired before the ball was in flight, the goal shall not count. If they agree that the period ended (as in Rule 5-8-c) before the foul occurred, the foul shall be disregarded unless it was intentional or flagrant. If the timers disagree, the goal shall count or the foul shall be penalized unless the referee has knowledge that alters such a ruling.

Officials and Their Duties

If an obvious error by the timer has occurred because of the failure to start or stop the game clock at the proper moment, the error may be corrected only when the referee has definite information relative to the time involved.

INTERPRETATIONS

Play 1: The signal to end the last period cannot be heard. The two officials disagree as to whether the ball was in flight during a try for field goal or whether a foul occurred before time expired.
Ruling: Final decision must be made by the referee. The timer will indicate if the ball was in flight before the buzzer sounded only if requested to do so by the referee. The referee will use his or her best judgment; but if the evidence for counting or not counting the goal or foul is equal, the referee will declare that it counts.

Play 2: (Men) The game clock indicates 1:13 left in the second half when Team A makes a throw-in after a charged timeout. Team A is charged with a 10-second violation, but the game clock shows only eight seconds were used. The timekeeper indicates the game clock started when the throw-in was touched on the court.
Ruling: Violation. B's ball out of bounds for a throw-in at the nearest spot. The referee is unlikely to know whether an error in starting the game clock has been made. Rule 2-10 does not provide for the correction of an error made in the referee's counting of seconds.

Play 3: As the official calls a five-second closely guarded violation, the official sounds the whistle and gives the signal to stop the game clock. The official is able to see the exact time remaining in the second half while doing this. The game clock shows five seconds remaining. The game clock is stopped: (a) at five seconds; or (b) at four seconds; or (c) at three seconds; or (d) the time runs out completely.

Ruling: In (a) there has been no obvious timing error. However, in (b), (c) and (d), more than one second of time has elapsed from the time the signal was given until the timing device was stopped. The referee will order five seconds put on the game clock. In all cases, the referee has definite information that the game clock showed five seconds and will instruct the timer to put that time on the clock.

Play 4: The timer properly sounds a warning signal 15 seconds before the timeout expires and a final signal when the timeout ends. The official administering the throw-in sounds the whistle to alert the players that the game will resume; however, neither team has left its huddle on the sideline.

Ruling: The official will place the ball at the throw-in spot and begin the throw-in count.

Play 5: The administering official has reached the five-second throw-in count on Team A after placing the ball on the floor when A was not ready to play after a timeout.

Ruling: The violation is administered and the ball is made available to Team B for a throw-in.

Play 6: After a timeout, the official administering a free throw has alerted players that the game will resume. (a) The free thrower is not ready; or (b) Team B is not occupying the bottom marked spaces.

Ruling: In (a), if A1 is in the semicircle and does not take the ball or is outside the semicircle, the ball is placed on the line and the count is started. A violation will result if the throw is not attempted in 10 seconds or if the free thrower enters the semicircle. If A1 is out-

Officials and Their Duties

side the circle, A1 cannot enter without violating. In (b), once the ball is placed at the disposal of A1, it will be an automatic delayed violation by B for not occupying the bottom marked space on each side. However, in (a) and (b), any player from Team A may request and be granted a timeout before the expiration of the 10-second time limit for shooting the free throw.

Play 7: Both teams remain in their huddles after a timeout even though the official administering the throw-in has alerted them that play will resume. (a) Before or (b) after the ball is placed at the spot, Team A or B indicates it desires a timeout.
Ruling: In (a), either team may request and be granted a timeout. In (b), only the team entitled to the throw-in may be granted a timeout after the throw-in count has been started.

Play 8: Team B is still huddling at the end of the half-time intermission. The administering official has properly alerted both teams that the game will resume.
Ruling: If there is undue delay of the game caused by Team B, a technical foul shall be assessed.

Section 13   **Duties of Shot-Clock Operator** A 35-second shot clock is used in men's basketball and a 30-second shot clock is used in women's basketball. The shot clock is used for the entire game, including overtime periods. The shot-clock operator shall control a separate timing device with a horn that shall have a sound distinct and different from that of the game clock. An alternate timing device shall be available. In addition, the shot-clock operator shall:

a. Start the timing device when a player inbounds gains possession of the ball on a throw-in or when a team initially gains possession of the ball from a jump ball, a rebound or a loose ball.

Duties of Shot-Clock Operator

b. Stop the timing device and reset it when team control is again established after the team loses possession of the ball [Note: The mere touching of the ball by an opponent does not start a new period if the same team remains in control of the ball.]; when a foul occurs; when a held ball occurs [except for 2-13-(c)-(4)]; when a try for the goal strikes the basket ring; or when a violation occurs.

c. Stop the timing device and continue time without a reset when play begins under the following circumstances:

(1) The ball is deflected out of bounds by a defensive player;

(2) A player is injured or loses a contact lens;

(3) A charged timeout has concluded; and

(4) During team control as defined in 4-7-(b), a defensive player causes a held ball and the possession arrow favors the offensive team.

The offensive team upon regaining possession of the ball for the throw-in shall have the unexpired time to attempt a shot. After leaving the player's hand, that attempt must strike the basket ring or enter the basket.

d. Sound the horn at the expiration of the shot-clock period. This does not stop play unless recognized by an official's whistle. If the shot clock indicates 00 but the horn has not sounded, time has not expired. The timing device shall be turned off when the game clock shows less time than a shot-clock period.

e. Allow the timing device to continue during a loose-ball situation if the offense retains possession or when a field-goal try is attempted at the wrong basket.

If there is doubt as to whether a score was made within the shot-clock period or whether a try for goal strikes the basket ring, the final decision shall be made by the game officials.

INTERPRETATIONS

Play 1: A1 touches the ball that was inbounded by A2. It strikes the floor and bounces on the floor until A3 gains control by dribbling the ball. The operator starts the shot clock when A1 touches the ball.
Ruling: The operator was wrong. Merely touching the ball does not establish player or team control. The shot clock should have started when A3 started the dribble because at that moment team control had been established.

Play 2: Official inadvertently blows the whistle and the shot-clock horn sounds while the ball, after being shot by A1, is in the air. How is play resumed if (a) shot is successful or (b) does not strike the basket ring or (c) strikes the basket ring but does not enter the basket?
Ruling: In (a), the whistle and shot-clock horn are ignored. In (b) and (c), play is resumed by the alternating-possession provision with clock reset at the full shot-clock period.

Play 3: A1 releases the ball on a try for goal. B1 partially blocks the shot and it (a) hits the rim; (b) goes out of bounds; or (c) goes through the net.
Ruling: In (a) and (c), play is legal and action continues. In (b), the official blows the whistle to stop play and the shot-clock operator stops but does not reset the shot clock. On the ensuing inbounds pass by Team A, the game clock starts when the inbounds pass touches any player on the court. The shot clock continues when a player from Team A gains possession or is reset when a player from Team B gains possession.

Rule 3

Players, Substitutes and Equipment

Rule 3

Players, Substitutes and Equipment

Section 1 **The Team** Each team consists of five players, one of whom is the captain. The game must start with five players but may continue with fewer than five players if all other squad members are not eligible to play. A team must continue to play with five players as long as it has that number available. When there is only one player participating for a team, that team shall forfeit the game unless the referee believes that both teams have an opportunity to win the game.

Section 2 **The Captain** The captain is the representative of the team and may address an official on matters of interpretation or to obtain essential information, if it is done in a courteous manner. Therefore, dialogue between coaches and officials should be kept to a bare minimum. Any player may address an official to request a timeout (Rule 5-10-c) or permission to leave the court.

INTERPRETATION

Play: Teams A and B each have cocaptains. At the pregame conference, one of the cocaptains requests permission from the referee that both cocaptains be allowed to confer with the officials on interpretations. **Ruling:** Cocaptains may participate in the pregame conference, but only one captain of each team may confer with the officials during the game. During the

Players, Substitutes and Equipment

pregame conference, the referee should be informed which captain of each team shall be the speaker during the game.

Section 3 **Lineup** At least 10 minutes before the scheduled starting time, each team shall supply the scorers with:

a. Names and numbers of squad members who may participate, and

b. The five starting players designated.

After the time limits specified have been reached, a team is charged with a maximum of one technical foul for one or more of the following:

c. Failure to comply with a or b;

d. Name(s) added to the squad list;

e. Change(s) in a squad member's number(s) without reporting the change(s) to the scorers and an official; and

f. Changes in the starting lineup, except when the changes are necessitated by obvious injury or illness or to replace a designated starter to shoot a technical foul free throw.

Once the game begins, a team is charged with a maximum of one technical foul regardless of the number of infractions of (a) through (f).

INTERPRETATIONS

Play 1: Nine minutes before the scheduled starting time for the game, Team A presents its squad roster and its starting lineup to the scorer and then, at six minutes before the game starting time, Team A presents four additional names to the scorer for the squad list.
Ruling: Team A is assessed one technical foul. Team B will be awarded the ball for a throw-in at the division line after the last free throw.

Substitutions

Play 2: Team A properly submits its squad list and designates its five starters in compliance with the rule before the starting time of the game. However, the number for each squad member is erroneously indicated. The error is not noted until approximately 1½ minutes have been played.

Ruling: A technical foul is charged to Team A. A player must wear the number indicated in the scorebook or change the scorebook number to that which he or she is wearing. If the squad member, before participating, changes the number he or she wears to that indicated in the scorebook, there is no penalty. If the number in the book for a player is changed before participation and the change is reported to both the scorer and an official, there is no penalty.

Section 4 **Substitutions** Substitutes who desire to enter shall report to the scorers, giving their numbers and the numbers of the players who are being replaced. Substitutions between halves shall be made to the official scorer by the substitute(s) or a team representative before the signal that ends the intermission. Substitutions during a timeout must report to or be in position to report to the scorer before the warning signal, which is sounded 15 seconds before the timeout ends. Substitutions may not occur after the warning signal to prepare to resume play. If entry is at any time other than between halves, and a substitute, who is entitled and ready to enter, reports to the scorers, the scorers shall sound the horn if (or as soon as) the ball is dead and time is out except after successful field goals in the last minute of the game and the last minute of any overtime. The substitute shall remain outside the boundary until beckoned by an official, whereupon the substitute shall enter immediately. If the ball is about to become live, the beckoning signal should be withheld. The entering player shall not replace a free thrower as stated in Rule 8-2. If the substitute enters to replace a player who is to attempt a free throw, the substitute shall withdraw until the next opportunity to substitute.

A player who has been withdrawn may not reenter before the next opportunity to substitute after the clock has been started properly after the player's replacement.

A legal substitute becomes a player when he or she legally enters the court. If a substitute enters illegally during a dead ball, the substitute becomes a player when the ball becomes live.

INTERPRETATIONS

Play 1: A1 is injured during a play in which A1 has been fouled. As a result, A1 cannot attempt the free throw awarded to him or her. Substitute A6 replaces A1 and attempts the free throw, which is successful. Substitute A7 replaces A6 before the clock starts.
Ruling: The procedure is legal.

Play 2: A technical foul is assessed against Team A. B6 replaces B1 and makes the second free-throw attempt. After the attempt, B1 desires to reenter.
Ruling: Illegal. B1 may not reenter before the next opportunity to substitute after the clock has started after his or her replacement. (Rule 8-2-b)

Play 3: During a dead ball, A6 replaces A5. Before the ball is put into play, a technical foul is assessed against Team B. A5 is designated by the coach to enter the game and attempt the free throws resulting from Team B's technical foul.
Ruling: A5 may not reenter to attempt the free throws because the game clock has not been started since A5 left the game.

Play 4: A1, who is designated as a starter 10 minutes before the scheduled starting time of the game, becomes ill one minute before the game is about to start.
Ruling: A1 may be replaced without a technical foul being assessed. Illness or injury is considered to be an extenuating and unavoidable situation that permits a substitution without penalty. A1 would be permitted to enter the game later if able.

Play 5: After a successful free throw, A1 enters the court before the throw-in, and A1's illegal entry is not detected until after the ball becomes live.
Ruling: A1 became a legal player when the ball became live. Because discovery of the infraction followed the ball becoming live, the infraction by A1 is ignored.

Play 6: After substitutions, the official lines up players to aid them in locating opponents.
Ruling: This shall be done at the request of a captain only when three or more substitutes for the same team enter during an opportunity to substitute.

Play 7: After a successful field goal with 48 seconds left on the game clock, the timer sounds the horn for substitute A6 to enter the game.
Ruling: Substitute A6 may not enter. While the clock is stopped after successful field goals in the last minute of play, the rule specifically states that no substitution is allowed. A team may request a timeout and then insert substitutions any time the ball is dead and the clock is stopped.

Section 5 **Shirts, Numbers, Uniforms**
a. Team shirts shall be of the same solid color front and back. For men, the shirts shall be tucked in the game pants. Beginning with the 1999-00 season, women must wear team shirts that can be tucked in the game pants. For women, a player's shirt designed to be

worn inside the game pants shall be tucked inside the game pants.
Note: The first time an official must tell a player to tuck in the shirt tail, the official will issue a warning to the head coach. The next time any player on the same team has the shirt tail out, that player must leave the game until the next opportunity to substitute.

The only decorations permitted are: (1) side inserts, including trim, of no more than 4 inches in width of any color centered vertically below the armpit and (2) piping not to exceed 1 inch around the neck and arm opening and (3) a waist opening band of any color not to exceed 4 inches wide and at least 4 inches below the bottom of the number or name if it appears under the number. Decorations such as mascots, stars, commemorative patches and logos of any kind are permissible on the game jersey only within the 4-inch side insert. Manufacturers' or distributors' labels or trademarks are not permitted on the team shirt. An undershirt is considered to be part of the shirt and must be a color similar to the shirt. In addition, the sleeves and neckline of undershirts shall be unaltered (e.g., no cut-off sleeves or cut necklines) and both sleeves must be of the same length. No logos, decorations, trim, commemorative patches, lettering or numbering may be used on an undershirt. An illegal undershirt may not be worn.

b. Tights that extend below the game pants must be similar in color to the pants.
c. No more than two identifying names or abbreviations of the names may be placed on either, or on both, the front and back of the shirt. The name(s) must conform to the following:

(1) It identifies the school, the school nickname

Shirts, Numbers, Uniforms

or mascot, or the player's name.

(2) Placement is vertical and/or horizontal.

(3) If horizontal, the lettering may be arched, but the first and last letters must be in the same horizontal plane.

(4) Tails above or below the lettering are not permitted.

(5) Placement must be such that the number(s) is clearly visible.

d. Each player shall be numbered on the front and back of the shirt with plain Arabic numerals.

> (1) The following numbers are legal: 0, 3, 4, 5, 00, 10, 11, 12, 13, 14, 15, 20, 21, 22, 23, 24, 25, 30, 31, 32, 33, 34, 35, 40, 41, 42, 43, 44, 45, 50, 51, 52, 53, 54, 55. Beginning with the 1996-97 season, team rosters can include 0 or 00 but not both.

(2) The number shall be at least 6 inches high on the back and at least 4 inches high on the front and not less than ¾-inch in width.

> (3) Beginning with the 1996-97 season, numbers shall be centered on the front and back of game jerseys.

(4) No more than three colors may be used. The style of the number must be clearly visible and conform to one of the following:

> (a) A solid contrasting color with no more than two solid ¼-inch borders. A solid contrasting "shadow" trim, not to exceed one-half inch in width, may be used on part of the uniform number. If the shirt color is used as a border, it must be counted as one of the allowed colors.

(b) The shirt color itself when bordered with not more than two ¼-inch solid border(s) contrasting with the shirt color.

e. Members of the same squad shall not wear identical numbers. If two or more squad members are wearing identical numbers, the second-listed squad member (and any following member) wearing an identical number is charged with a technical foul. The penalty shall be imposed whenever the infraction is discovered. When there is duplication, only one squad member will be permitted to wear a given number. All others must change to a number not already in use before they may participate.

f. Uniforms (except game jerseys and T-shirts) and all other items of apparel (e.g., warm-ups, socks, headbands, wristbands and towels) may bear only a single manufacturer's or distributor's normal label or trademark not to exceed 2¼-square inches, including any additional material (e.g., patch) surrounding the normal trademark or logo. In addition, the normal label or trademark must be contained within a four-sided geometrical figure (i.e., rectangle, square, parallelogram). For example, if a manufacturer's trademark or logo fits within a 2¼-inch by 1-inch rectangle, the logo would be permissible, inasmuch as it does not exceed the 2¼-square-inch area requirement.

INTERPRETATIONS

Play 1: May a player buy his or her way into a game by being assessed a technical foul for wearing an illegal undershirt or undergarment?
Ruling: Illegal undershirts or undergarments, like jewelry, may not be worn. The illegal apparel must be removed in order to play.

Players' Equipment

Play 2: Contesting teams have uniforms of the same color.
Ruling: If possible, each team should have two sets of uniforms, one of light color and the other dark. The light color is for home games. The team that violates this policy should change. If there is doubt, the officials should request the home team to change; on a neutral floor, the officials decide.

Play 3: A game official detects that A1's team shirt is not tucked in the game pants.
Ruling: The first time an official must tell a player to tuck in the shirt tail, the official issues a warning to the head coach. The next time any player on the same team has the shirt tail out, that player must leave the game until the next opportunity to substitute. (**Exception:** For women, shirts designed to be worn outside the game pants may remain outside. Those uniform shirts designed to be tucked in the game pants must be tucked in. Beginning in 1999-00, women's teams must wear team shirts that can be tucked in the game pants.)

Section 6 **Players' Equipment** The referee shall not permit any player to wear equipment that in his or her judgment is dangerous to other players. Elbow, hand, finger, wrist or forearm guards, casts or braces made of plaster, metal or any other nonpliable substance, shall be prohibited. Pliable (soft) plastic may be used as protective covering for an injury. The prohibition of the use of hard-substance material does not apply to the upper arm, shoulder, thigh or lower leg if the material is padded so as not to create a hazard for other players.

Equipment that could cut or cause an injury to another player is prohibited, without respect to whether or not the equipment is hard. Excessively long fingernails are not permitted.

Players, Substitutes and Equipment

Head decorations, head wear and jewelry are illegal. Headbands no wider than two inches made of nonabrasive, unadorned, single-color cloth, elastic, fiber, soft leather, pliable plastic or rubber are legal.

Any equipment that is unnatural and designed to increase a player's height or reach, or to gain an advantage, shall not be used.

Equipment used must be appropriate for basketball. Basketball knee braces may be worn if they are properly covered. A protector for a broken nose, even though made of hard material, is permissible if it does not endanger other players. Eyeglass protectors are appropriate equipment if they meet the qualifications outlined in this rule.

INTERPRETATION

Play: Substitute A6 enters the court and is wearing jewelry, an illegal headpiece or a hat.
Ruling: The official shall order this player to remove the illegal equipment. A6 may not enter wearing jewelry or a hat. The player cannot buy his or her way into the game by accepting a technical foul. If a player is wearing jewelry in a game, the player shall remove the jewelry immediately or be required to leave the game.

Rule 4

Definitions

Rule 4

Definitions

Section 1 **Basket** A basket is the 18-inch ring, its flange and braces, and appended net through which players attempt to throw the ball. A team's own basket is the one into which its players try to throw the ball.

> Teams shall warm up and shoot during the first half at the basket farthest from their bench area. The teams shall change baskets for the second half.

If the official(s) erroneously permits a team to go in the wrong direction, when the error is discovered (1) all points scored, (2) fouls committed and (3) time consumed shall count as though each team had gone in the proper direction. Play shall be resumed with each team going in the proper direction based on pregame choice.

Section 2 **Basket Interference** Basket interference occurs when a player touches the ball or any part of the basket while the ball is on or within the basket, touches the ball while any part of it is within the imaginary cylinder that has the basket ring as its lower base, or reaches through the basket from below and touches the ball before it enters the cylinder.

Section 3 **Blocking, Charging**
a. Blocking is illegal personal contact that impedes the progress of an opponent.
b. Charging is illegal personal contact by pushing or moving into an opponent's torso.

Section 4 **Bonus Free Throw** A bonus free throw is a second free throw that is awarded for each common foul (except a player-control foul) committed by a player of a team, beginning with that team's seventh foul in a half, which is a combination of personal, unsporting and contact technical fouls, provided the first free throw for the foul is successful. For men, beginning with the 10th foul in a half, which is a combination of personal, unsporting and contact technical fouls, two free throws are awarded for each common foul (except a player-control foul). A player-control foul also is counted as a team foul for reaching the bonus. All unsporting technical fouls charged to anyone on the bench count toward the team foul total and bonus free-throw situations.

| Section 5 | **Boundary Lines** Boundary lines of the court consist of end and side lines. The inside edges of these lines define the inbounds and out-of-bounds areas. |

| Section 6 | **Closely Guarded** A player is closely guarded when holding (not dribbling) the ball while being guarded within six feet anywhere on the court for women and in the front court only for men. |

| Section 7 | **In Control—Player, Team**
a. A player is in control when holding a live ball or dribbling it while inbounds.
b. A team is in control when a player of the team is in control and also while a live ball is being passed between teammates. Team control continues until the ball is in flight during a try for goal, or an opponent secures control or the ball becomes dead. There is no team control during a jump ball or a throw-in, during the tapping of a rebound, after the ball is in flight during a try for goal, during the period that follows any of these acts while the ball is being batted (from the vicinity of other players) in an attempt to secure control, or during a dead ball. In these situations, team control is |

Dribble

reestablished when a player secures control.

c. Control for purposes of establishing the alternating-possession procedure occurs when:

(1) A player is in control.

(2) The ball is handed to or placed at the disposal of the free thrower after a common foul.

(3) The ball is handed to or placed at the disposal of the thrower-in.

INTERPRETATION

Play: (Men) With A1 in his team's backcourt and being pressured by B1 during an attempt to advance the ball, the official has reached a seven count on A1. At this point, while A1 is still dribbling, B1 touches the ball and it goes back toward B's basket. A1 retrieves the ball and continues to dribble.

Ruling: There has been no change in team control, and the 10-second count continues.

Section 8 **Disposal of Ball** The ball is at the disposal of a player when it is:

a. Handed to a thrower-in or free thrower.

b. Caught by the free thrower after it is bounced to him or her.

c. Placed at a spot on the floor.

d. Available to a player after a goal.

Section 9 **Disqualified Player** A disqualified player is one who is barred from further participation in the game because of committing a fifth foul, including personal, unsporting and contact technical fouls; a flagrant foul; or for an infraction of Rule 10-3-a or b and 10-7-(d).

Section 10 **Dribble** A dribble is ball movement caused by a player in control who bats, pushes or taps the ball to the floor once or several times. During a dribble, the ball may be batted into the air, provided it is permitted to strike the floor one or more times before the ball is touched again with the hands.

The dribble may be started by pushing, throwing, tapping or batting the ball to the floor. The dribble ends when:

a. The dribbler catches or causes the ball to come to rest with one or both hands.
b. The dribbler touches the ball with both hands simultaneously.
c. An opponent bats the ball.
d. The ball becomes dead.

An interrupted dribble occurs when the ball is loose after deflecting off the dribbler or after it momentarily gets away from the dribbler. During an interrupted dribble, the following cannot occur:

e. Three-second lane violation.
f. Player-control foul.
g. Acknowledgement of a timeout request.

INTERPRETATIONS

Play 1: A1, while advancing the ball by dribbling, manages to keep a hand in contact with the ball until it reaches its maximum height. A1 maintains such control as the ball descends, pushing it to the floor at the last moment; however, after six or seven bounces, A1's hands are in contact with the ball and the palm of the hand on this particular dribble is skyward.
Ruling: Violation. The ball has come to rest on the hand while the palm and the fingers are facing upward and the dribble has ended. If the player continues to move or stand still and dribble, the player has committed a violation by dribbling a second time. (Rules 4-10-a and 9-6.)

Dribble

Play 2: Is a player dribbling while tapping the ball during a jump, when a pass rebounds from the player's hand, when the player fumbles or when the player taps a rebound or pass away from other players who are attempting to get it?
Ruling: No. The player is not in control under these conditions.

Play 3: A1 receives a pass from A2 and comes to a stop legally with the right foot established as the pivot foot. A1 tosses the ball from one hand to the other several times and then proceeds to bat the ball to the floor before A1 lifts the pivot foot.
Ruling: Legal.

Play 4: A1 dribbles and comes to a stop, after which A1 throws the ball: (a) against the opponent's backboard and catches the rebound; or (b) against the official, immediately recovering the ball and dribbling again.
Ruling: A1 has committed a violation in both (a) and (b). Throwing the ball against an opponent's backboard or an official constitutes another dribble, provided A1 is first to touch the ball after it strikes the official or the board.

Play 5: In the front court of A (the backcourt of B), A1 passes the ball to A2. B1, in an attempt to secure the ball, bats it well down court toward B's basket. The ball bounces several times before B1 can recover it in B's front court. B1 then dribbles to B's basket and scores.
Ruling: Legal. The bat of the ball by B1, is not considered part of the dribble. B1 does not have control of the ball until securing it after batting it.

Play 6: A1 is dribbling the ball when: (a) A1 bats the ball over the head of an opponent, runs around the opponent, taps the ball to the floor and continues to

dribble or (b) A1 fumbles the ball in an attempt to complete his or her dribble and causes the ball to roll out of reach so that A1 must run to recover it.
Ruling: Violation in (a) because it is touched twice during a dribble, before it touches the floor. In (b), it is illegal to continue to dribble but A1 may recover the ball.

Play 7: Is it a dribble when a player stands still and (a) bounces the ball or (b) holds the ball and touches it on the floor once or more?
Ruling: (a) Yes. (b) No.

Play 8: A1 is dribbling the ball in the front court when the ball momentarily gets away from him or her. While the dribble is interrupted: (a) A1 pushes B2 while trying to retrieve the ball; (b) A2 is in the lane for four seconds; and (c) A1 calls a timeout.
Ruling: (a) Common foul called on A1; (b) lane violations are not in effect during an interrupted dribble; and (c) a timeout may not be acknowledged during an interrupted dribble.

Section 11 **Dunking** Dunking occurs when any player gains control of a ball that is neither in the cylinder nor on the rim and then attempts to drive, force or stuff the ball through the basket.

Section 12 **Extra Period** An extra period is the extension of playing time allocated to break a tie score. The length of each extra period is five minutes.

Section 13 **Fighting** In the opinion of the official, if any flagrant foul is deemed to be a fight, the fighting penalty is invoked. This could include, but is not exclusive to, an attempt to strike an opponent with the arms, hands, legs or feet, or a combative action by one or more players, a coach or team personnel. Combative action includes but is not exclusive to:

a. A player, coach or other team personnel attempting to punch or kick an opponent; whether there is contact with an opponent is irrelevant.

b. A player, coach or other team personnel who, in the opinion of a game official, instigates a fight by perpetrating an unsporting act toward an opponent that causes the opponent to retaliate by fighting.

Section 14 **Foul** A foul is an infraction of the rules that is charged to a squad member or a coach and is penalized in various ways. Following are the types of fouls (see Rule 10):

a. **Personal foul.** A personal foul is a foul committed by an active player that involves illegal contact with an opponent while the ball is live. A common foul is a personal foul that is neither flagrant nor intentional, nor committed against a player trying for a field goal, nor part of a double or multiple foul. (See Rule 10 for an expanded definition of a personal foul and for personal-foul penalties.)

b. **Technical foul.** A technical foul is a foul by any player (active or not active), coach or other team attendant that does not involve contact with an opponent or causes contact with an opponent while the ball is dead. Examples of technical fouls include unsporting conduct (acts of deceit, disrespect for opponents or officials; using vulgarity, profanity or obscene gestures whether or not they are directed at someone), calling an excessive timeout and hanging on the rim. (See Rule 10 for an expanded definition of a technical foul and for technical-foul penalties.)

c. **Flagrant foul.** A flagrant foul is a personal foul that involves violent contact with an opponent. Such contact includes striking with the elbow, kicking, kneeing, moving under a player who is in the air or crouching or hipping in a manner that might cause severe injury to the opponent. A flagrant foul also is a technical foul when it involves unsporting conduct or contact while the ball is dead. (See Rule 10 for flagrant-foul penalties and an explanation of the fighting rule.)

d. Intentional foul. An intentional foul is a personal foul that, on the basis of observation of the act, is not a legitimate attempt to directly play the ball or a player. Judgment is not based upon severity of the act. Contact with the thrower-in shall be ruled an intentional foul. Holding or pushing an opponent in full view of an official in order to stop play or pushing a player in the back to prevent a score when there is no possibility of getting into position to guard, are equally intentional. A foul also shall be ruled intentional, if while playing the ball, a player causes excessive contact with an opponent. (See Rule 10 for intentional-foul penalties.)

e. Player-control foul. A player-control foul is a common foul committed:

> (1) Men—by a player when he is in control of the ball.
>
> (2) Women—by a player when she is in control of the ball or by an airborne shooter.

A player-control foul cannot occur during an interrupted dribble. Free throws are not awarded when a player-control foul is committed; however, a player-control foul counts toward a player's five fouls for disqualification and toward team fouls for the bonus situation.

INTERPRETATIONS

Play 1: (Women) A1 ends the dribble and passes the ball to A2: (a) while the ball is in the air; or (b) after A2 has control, A1 charges into B2.

Ruling: The foul on A1 in both (a) and (b) is not a player-control foul as A1 was not holding or dribbling the ball and was not an airborne shooter in either situation. In (a), if the official is in doubt as to whether the charging occurred before or after the ball was released on the pass, it should not be ruled a player-control foul.

Play 2: (Women) Is it possible for airborne shooter A1 to commit a foul that would not be player control?
Ruling: Yes. The airborne shooter could be charged with an intentional or flagrant personal foul or with a technical foul. None of these fouls can be player control. If such a foul occurs, it is penalized as dictated by the type of foul.

Play 3: (Women) Airborne A1 is fouled by B1 during a try for a field goal. A1 releases the ball then illegally contacts B2 in returning to the floor after the shot. The ball goes through the basket.
Ruling: The situation is a false double foul. The foul by B1 did not cause the ball to become dead since A1 had started the trying motion. However, airborne shooter A1's foul is a player-control foul that does cause the ball to become dead immediately. No goal can be scored even if the ball already had gone through the basket before the foul. Since the goal is unsuccessful, A1 is awarded two free throws for the foul by B1. No players are allowed in lane spaces as Team B will be awarded the ball after the last free throw. If the last throw is successful, the throw-in is from anywhere along the end line. If the last throw is unsuccessful, the throw-in is from a designated spot nearest the foul. The situation is a false double foul.

Definitions

Other less common types of fouls include:

f. Double personal foul. A double personal foul is a situation in which two opponents commit personal fouls against each other at approximately the same time.

g. Double technical foul. A double technical foul is a situation in which opponents commit technical fouls against each other at approximately the same time.

See page 164 for a summary of the administration of penalties for double fouls.

h. False double foul. A false double foul is a situation in which there are fouls by both teams, the second of which occurs before the clock is started after the first but such that at least one of the attributes of a double foul is absent.

INTERPRETATIONS

Play 1: B1 commits a common foul on A1 before the bonus rule is in effect for either team. The ball is awarded to Team A at the nearest out-of-bounds spot. A2 fouls B2 during the throw-in before the clock is started. Team B is in the bonus situation.
Ruling: Foul by A2 results in a false-double-foul situation. B2 is awarded a one-and-one. If both throws are successful, the ball is awarded to A for a throw-in at the end line from any point out of bounds. If either free throw is missed, the ball is in play if it touches the ring. (Rule 8-6)

Play 2: Player A1 is entitled to a one-and-one free throw. Before the ball is handed to A1, Team A's coach is assessed a technical foul.
Ruling: The technical foul creates a false-double-foul situation. Team B is awarded two free throws because

Front Court and Backcourt

of the technical by the coach. Team B will shoot two free throws after A1 attempts a one-and-one, and then the ball is awarded to Team B out of bounds at the division line.

i. Multiple foul. A multiple foul is a situation in which two or more teammates commit personal fouls against the same opponent at approximately the same time. A false multiple foul is a situation in which there are two or more fouls by the same team and such that the last foul is committed before the clock is started after the first, and such that at least one of the attributes of a multiple foul is absent.

Section 15 **Free Throw** A free throw is the privilege given a player to score one point by an unhindered try for goal from within the free-throw semicircle and behind the free-throw line. A free throw starts when the ball is given to the free thrower at the free-throw line or is placed on the line. It ends when: the try is successful, it is certain the try will not be successful, when the try touches the floor or any player, or when the ball becomes dead.

Section 16 **Front Court and Backcourt**
a. A team's front court consists of that part of the court between its end line and the nearer edge of the division line and including its basket and the inbounds part of its backboard.
b. A team's backcourt consists of the rest of the court, including its opponent's basket and inbounds part of the backboard and the entire division line.
c. A live ball is in the front court or backcourt of the team in control as follows:

(1) A ball that is in contact with a player or with the court is in the backcourt if either the ball or

Definitions

the player (either player if the ball is touching more than one) is touching the backcourt. It is in the front court if neither the ball nor the player is touching the backcourt.

(2) A ball that is not in contact with a player or the court retains the same status as when it was last in contact with a player or the court.

(3) During a dribble from backcourt to front court, the ball is in the front court when both feet of the dribbler and the ball touch the court entirely in the front court.

Section 17   **Fumble**   A fumble is the accidental loss of player control by unintentionally dropping the ball or permitting it to slip from one's grasp.

Section 18   **Goaltending**   Goaltending occurs when a player touches the ball during a field-goal try or tap while the ball is in its downward flight and the entire ball is above the level of the ring and has the possibility of entering the basket in flight but is not touching an imaginary cylinder that has the basket ring as its lower base. It is goaltending to touch the ball outside the cylinder during a free-throw attempt, regardless of whether the attempt is on its upward or downward flight.

Section 19   **Guarding**   Guarding is the act of legally placing the body in the path of an offensive opponent. There is no minimum distance required between the guard and opponent, but the maximum is six feet when closely guarded. The six-foot distance applies only when a player is holding the ball. Every player is entitled to a spot on the floor provided such players get there first without illegally contacting an opponent. It is assumed

Hands and Arms, Legal Use of

the guard may shift to maintain guarding position in the path of the dribbler provided the guard does not charge into the dribbler nor otherwise cause contact as outlined in Rule 10-10. The responsibility of the dribbler for contact is not shifted merely because the guard turns or ducks to absorb shock when contact caused by the dribbler is imminent.

a. To establish an initial legal guarding position on the player with the ball:

    (1) The guard must have both feet touching the floor. If the guard jumps into position initially, both feet must return to the floor after the jump, before the guard has established a guarding position.

    (2) The guard's torso must be facing the opponent.

    (3) No time and distance are required.

    (4) If the opponent with the ball is airborne, the guard must have established legal position before the opponent left the floor.

b. To establish legal guarding position on a player without the ball:

    (1) Time and distance are factors required to establish an initial legal position.

    (2) The guard must give the opponent the time and distance to avoid contact.

    (3) The distance need not be more than two strides.

    (4) If the opponent is airborne, the guard must have established legal position before the opponent left the floor.

Section 20 — Hands and Arms, Legal Use of

a. The arms may be extended vertically above the shoulder and need not be lowered to avoid contact with an opponent when the action of the opponent causes contact. This legal use of the arms and hands usually occurs when guarding the thrower-in, the player with the ball in pressing tactics and a player with the ball who is maneuvering to try for goal by pivoting, jumping or hooking.

b. Reaching to block or slap the ball controlled by a dribbler, a thrower for goal, or a player holding the ball, and accidentally hitting the hand of the opponent when it is in contact with the ball, is legal use of the hands.

c. A player may hold the hands and arms in front of his or her face or body for protection and to absorb force from an imminent charge by an opponent. This same protective use of the arms and hands occurs when a player who has set a blind screen is about to be run into by the player being screened. The action, however, should be a recoil action rather than a pushing action.

d. A player may not use the arms, hands, hips or shoulders to force his or her way through a screen or to hold the screener and then push the screener aside in order to maintain a guarding position relative to his or her opponent.

e. Extending the arms fully or partially other than vertically so that the freedom of movement of an opponent is hindered when contact with the arms occurs is not legal. The extension of the elbow when the hands are on the hips, when the hands are held near the chest or when the arms are held more or less horizontally are examples of legal positions. These positions are employed when rebounding, screening or in the various aspects of post play.

Section 21 **Held Ball** A held ball occurs when an opponent places his or her hand(s):

a. So firmly on the ball that control cannot be obtained without undue roughness.

b. On the ball to prevent an airborne player from throwing the ball or attempting a try.

INTERPRETATION

Play: A1 leaves the floor to attempt a try for goal. B1 jumps to defend against the try and (a) touches the ball before it leaves A1's hand and A1 returns to the floor with the ball and the ball never loses contact with A1's hand(s) or (b) the ball loses contact with A1's hand(s), A1 retrieves the ball while in the air and returns to the floor in possession of the ball and begins to dribble or (c) after the ball touches the floor, A1 recovers the ball and begins to dribble.

Ruling: In (a) the official shall call a held ball. In (b) and (c) the play is legal. A1 has gained new possession in both instances.

Section 22 **Holding** Holding is illegal personal contact with an opponent that interferes with the opponent's freedom of movement.

Section 23 **Incidental Contact**

a. The mere fact that contact occurs does not constitute a foul. When 10 players are moving rapidly in a limited area, some contact is certain to occur.

b. Contact that is entirely incidental to an effort by an opponent to reach a loose ball, or incidental contact that may result when opponents are in equally favorable positions to perform normal defensive or offensive movements, should not be considered illegal even though the contact may be violent.

c. Similarly, contact that does not hinder the opponent from participating in normal defensive or offensive movements should be considered incidental. In cases of blind screens, the opponent may make inadvertent contact with the screener; and, if the opponent is running rapidly, the contact may be severe. Such a case

Definitions

is to be ruled as incidental contact provided the opponent stops (or attempts to stop) on contact and moves around the screen, and provided the screener is not displaced if he or she has the ball.

d. However, if a player approaches an opponent from behind or from a position from which the player has no reasonable chance to play the ball without making contact with the opponent, the responsibility is on the player in the unfavorable position.

Section 24 **Jump Ball** A jump ball is a method of putting the ball into play by tossing it up between two opponents at mid-court. It begins when the ball leaves the official's hand and ends as outlined in Rule 6-4-b. A jump ball is used to begin the game and to begin overtime periods.

Section 25 **Location of a Player** The location of a player (or nonplayer) is determined by where he or she is touching the floor, as far as being inbounds or out of bounds or being in the front court or backcourt is concerned. When a player is in the air from a leap (except during a throw-in) or when a defensive player intercepts a ball while in the air, the player's status with reference to these two factors is the same as at the time the player was last in contact with the floor or an extension of the floor, such as a bleacher. When the ball touches an official, it is the same as touching the floor at the official's location.

INTERPRETATION

Play: Official is in the front court when the official runs into a pass thrown by A1 from A's backcourt. After touching the official, the ball (a) goes out of bounds or (b) rebounds to the backcourt, where it is recovered by A3.

Ruling: Touching the official is the same as touching the floor where the official is standing. In (a), ball is awarded to B for a throw-in. In (b), since A1 was the last player to touch the ball before it went into the backcourt, A1 caused it to go there. Backcourt violation. (Rule 9-11)

Section 26 **Multiple Throw** A multiple throw is a succession of free throws attempted by the same team.

Section 27 **Pass** A pass is movement of the ball caused by a player who throws, bats or rolls the ball to another player.

Section 28 **Penalty** A penalty for a foul is the charging of the offender with the foul and awarding one or more free throws, or awarding the ball to the opponents for a throw-in. The penalty for a violation is the awarding of the ball to the opponents for a throw-in, one or more points or a substitute free throw.

Section 29 **Pivot** A pivot takes place when a player who is holding the ball steps once or more than once in any direction with the same foot, while the other foot, called the pivot foot, is kept at its point of contact with the floor.

Section 30 **Rule** A rule is one of the groups of laws that govern the game. A game law (commonly called a rule) sometimes states or implies the ball is dead or a foul or violation is involved. If it does not, it is assumed the ball is live and no foul or violation has occurred to affect the given situation. A single infraction is not complicated by a second infraction unless so stated or implied.

Section 31 **Screen** A screen is legal action by a player who, without causing contact, delays or prevents an opponent from

Definitions

reaching a desired position. In screening tactics, the screener is not required to face any particular direction at any time. Leaning into the path of an opponent or extending the hips into the path, even though the feet are stationary, is not considered to be a stationary position. A player with the ball may be a screener and is subject to these principles. While most screening is by the offense, these principles apply equally to the defense.

Section 32 **Shot-Clock Try** A shot-clock try for field goal is defined as the ball having left the player's hand(s) before the sounding of the shot-clock horn and subsequently striking the basket ring or entering the basket.

Section 33 **Tap** A tap is considered a try for field goal. It is an attempt by a player to score two or three points by tapping the ball into his or her basket. The tap starts when the player's hand(s) or finger(s) touch the ball in an attempt to tap it into his or her basket. The tap ends when it is successful, when it is certain the tap is unsuccessful, when the ball touches the floor or when the ball becomes dead.

Section 34 **Throw-in** A throw-in is a method of putting the ball in play from out of bounds in accordance with Rules 7-3 through 7-6. The thrower-in is the player who attempts to make the throw-in. The player has five seconds to complete the throw-in. The throw-in begins when the ball is at the disposal of the player or team entitled to it. The throw-in count ends when the ball is released by the thrower-in so that the ball goes directly into the court. Throwing the ball to a teammate along the end line after a score does not constitute the end of the throw-in. The throw-in ends when the passed ball touches or is touched by an inbounds player other than the thrower-in. After a

Traveling

goal is scored by an opponent or awarded because of basket interference or goaltending, a player may run along the end line and/or pass to a teammate out of bounds before releasing the ball for a throw-in.

Section 35 **Traveling** Running with the ball (traveling) is moving a foot or the feet in any direction in excess of prescribed limits while holding the ball inbounds. The limits are as follows;:

a. A player who catches the ball with both feet on the floor may pivot, using either foot. When one foot is lifted, the other is the pivot foot.

b. A player who catches the ball while moving or dribbling may stop and establish a pivot foot as follows:

(1) If both feet are off the floor and the player lands:

(a) Simultaneously on both feet, either foot may be the pivot;

(b) On one foot followed by the other, the first foot to touch is the pivot;

(c) On one foot, the player may jump off that foot and simultaneously land on both; neither foot can be a pivot.

(2) If one foot is on the floor:

(a) It is the pivot when the other foot touches in a step;

(b) The player may jump off that foot and simultaneously land on both; neither foot can then be a pivot.

c. After coming to a stop and establishing a pivot foot:

(1) The pivot foot may be lifted, but not returned to the floor, before the ball is released on a pass or try for goal;

(2) The pivot foot may not be lifted, before the

Definitions

  ball is released, to start a dribble.
d. After coming to a stop when neither foot can be a pivot:
   (1) One or both feet may be lifted, but may not be returned to the floor, before the ball is released on a pass or try for goal;
   (2) Neither foot may be lifted, before the ball is released, to start a dribble.

INTERPRETATIONS

Play 1: A1 attempts to catch the ball while running rapidly. A1 fumbles the ball and succeeds in securing it before it strikes the floor. A1 then begins a dribble, taking several steps between the time A1 first touched the ball until catching it.
Ruling: There has been no violation provided A1 released the ball to start the dribble before the pivot foot was lifted from the floor after catching the ball.

Play 2: Is it traveling when (a) a player falls to the floor while holding the ball; or (b) gains control of the ball while on the floor and then because of momentum rolls or slides, after which the player passes or starts a dribble before getting to his or her feet?
Ruling: In (a), yes, because it is virtually impossible not to move the pivot foot when falling to the floor. In (b), no. If a player rises to his or her feet while holding the ball, a traveling violation has occurred. If a player falls to one knee while holding the ball, it is traveling if the pivot foot moves.

Play 3: A1 jumps to throw the ball. B1 prevents the throw by placing one or both hands on the ball and: (a) A1, or (b) A1 and B1 both return to the floor holding it.
Ruling: Held ball. However, if A1 voluntarily drops

Try for Field Goal

the ball before returning to the floor and then touches the ball before it is touched by another player, A1 has committed a violation for the illegal start of a dribble.

Section 36 **Try for Field Goal**

a. A try for field goal is an attempt by a player to score two or three points by throwing or tapping the ball into his or her basket. The try starts when the player begins the motion that habitually precedes the release of the ball. It is not essential that the ball leave the player's hand. The arm might be held so that the player cannot throw, yet he or she may be making an attempt. The tap starts when the player's hand(s) or finger(s) touch the ball in an attempt to tap it into his or her basket. The try or tap ends when the throw is successful, it is certain the throw is unsuccessful, when the thrown ball touches the floor or when the ball becomes dead. A dunk shot is a try.

Note: When play is to be resumed by a throw-in or a free throw is being administered and three-tenths (.3) of a second or less remains on the game or shot clock, a player may not gain possession of the ball and try for a field goal. The player can only tap the ball toward his/her basket to legally score a field goal. This does not apply to game or shot clocks that do not display tenths of a second.

b. The act of shooting begins simultaneously with the start of the try or tap and ends when the ball is clearly in flight.

Exception (Men): An airborne shooter who is fouled by an opponent while in the air but after the ball is released on a try or tap is considered to be in the act of shooting until both of the airborne shooter's feet return to the floor.

Definitions

c. (Women) An airborne shooter is a player who has released the ball on a try for goal or tap and has not returned to the floor.

INTERPRETATIONS

Play 1: B1 commits a common foul by holding A1 during a field-goal try but after A1 has completed the act of shooting (see airborne shooter exception for men in Rule 4-36-b). The foul occurs before the bonus rule applies. The attempt is: (a) successful or (b) unsuccessful.
Ruling: A personal foul is charged to B1 in both (a) and (b) but no free throw is awarded A1 in either case. In both (a) and (b), the ball is awarded to Team A at the out-of-bounds spot closest to where the foul occurred.

Play 2: A1 becomes confused and shoots the ball at the wrong basket. A1 is fouled while trying to shoot the ball and the ball goes in the basket. Is this a successful basket? If A1 missed, would A1 be granted two free throws for the foul by the B player?
Ruling: No goal. Ball became dead when the foul occurred. When a player shoots at the opponent's basket, it is not a try. If the team were in the bonus when the B player fouled A1, A1 would be given a one-and-one attempt. If Team A were not in the bonus, then the ball would be awarded to Team A at the nearest out-of-bounds spot.

Play 3: A1 attempts a try at A's basket after having completed the dribble. The try does not touch the backboard or the rim or any other player. A1 runs and is able to catch the ball before it strikes the floor. Is this traveling?
Ruling: When A1 recovered his or her own try, A1 could either dribble, pass or try again. There was no

team control by either team as soon as the try was airborne. However, if the shot clock expires and a try by A1 or a teammate has not struck the basket ring, it is a violation of the shot-clock rule.

Section 37 **Verticality** Verticality applies to a legal position. The basic components of the principle of verticality are:

a. Legal guarding position must be established and attained initially, and movement thereafter must be legal.

b. From this position, the defender may rise or jump vertically and occupy the space within his or her vertical plane.

c. The hands and arms of the defender may be raised within his or her vertical plane while the defender is on the floor or in the air.

d. The defender should not be penalized for leaving the floor vertically or having his or her hands and arms extended within the vertical plane.

e. The offensive player whether on the floor or airborne may not "clear out" or cause contact that is a foul.

f. The defender may not "belly up" or use the lower part of the body or arms to cause contact outside his or her vertical plane.

g. The player with the ball is to be given no more protection or consideration than the defender in the judging of which player has violated the rules.

Section 38 **Violation** A violation is a rule infraction of the type listed in Rule 9.

Rule 5

Scoring and Timing Regulations

Rule 5

Scoring and Timing Regulations

Section 1 **Goal—Definition** A goal is made when a live ball enters the basket from above and remains in or passes through except on a throw-in. Whether the clock is running or stopped has no influence on the counting of a goal. For women, if a player-control foul occurs after a goal, the goal is canceled.

INTERPRETATION

Play: A pass or a try for field goal by A1 comes down several feet in front of the basket. The ball strikes the floor without touching any player and bounces into the basket. Are two points counted for Team A: (a) if not complicated by expiration of time in a period or by a foul occurring while the ball is in flight; or (b) if time expires while the ball is in flight or a foul occurs while the ball is in flight?
Ruling: In (a), two points are scored. The try for field goal by A1 ends when the ball touches the floor but a field goal is sometimes scored when, technically, it is not the result of a try. The points count for the proper team. In the case cited, it is customary to credit the two points to A1. In (b), no points are scored. Neither the expiration of time nor a foul causes the ball to become dead immediately during a try for a field goal. During a pass, the ball becomes dead as a result of the foul or expiration of time. (Rule 4-36)

Scoring and Timing Regulations

Section 2 **Scoring** A successful try from the field beyond the three-point line counts three points for the team into whose basket the ball is thrown. A goal from the field other than from the three-point area counts two points for the team into whose basket the ball is thrown. A goal from a free throw is credited to the thrower and counts one point for the thrower's team. If a player scores a field goal in the opponent's basket it shall count two points for the opponent. It is not credited to a player but is indicated in a footnote. The only infractions for which points are awarded are goaltending by the defense or basket interference at the opponent's basket.

Note 1: For a successful three-point field goal, the player must have one or both feet on the floor and be beyond the three-point line when the player attempts the shot. After the release of the ball, the shooter may land on the line or in any part of the two-point area. Touching the line places the shooter in the two-point area. There is no relation to the plane regarding the position of the shooter.

Note 2: When play is to be resumed by a throw-in or a free throw is being administered and three-tenths (.3) of a second or less remains on the game or shot clock, a player may not gain possession of the ball and try for a field goal. The player can only tap the ball toward his or her basket to legally score a field goal. This does not apply to game or shot clocks that do not display tenths of a second.

INTERPRETATIONS

Play 1: A2 receives the tap by A1 on center jump to start the extra period. A2 is confused and dribbles toward the basket that Team A had during the first half and dunks the ball legally into Team B's basket. **Ruling:** Legal goal. Two points are awarded to Team B. Ball is awarded to Team A out of bounds at the basket of Team B, and A may put the ball in play from anywhere at the end line as after any score by B (earned or awarded).

Play 2: With two-tenths (.2) of a second remaining on the game clock, Team A is awarded a throw-in at midcourt. A1 passes the ball to A2 who (a) catches the ball with both hands while in the air and throws the ball into his or her basket or (b) does not catch the ball but taps it into the basket. In both (a) and (b), the ball is in the air on the way to the basket when the game-ending horn sounds.
Ruling: In (a) the score does not count. With three-tenths (.3) of a second or less remaining on the game clock or shot clock, if the ball is to be put in play by a throw-in, a player can only tap the ball toward the basket to successfully score a field goal. Despite the ball being in the air before the horn sounded, the official must disallow the basket. In (b), the basket counts.

Section 3   **Winning Team** The winning team is the one that has accumulated the greater number of points when the game ends.

Section 4   **Forfeited Game** If a forfeit is declared while a game is in progress, the score shall be recorded as 2-0 and all statistics (other than won-lost and coach's records) are voided, unless 30 minutes of playing time has been completed. If 30 minutes of playing time has been completed, the score shall stand and all statistics shall count. If the team that is behind is to be declared the winner, the score will be marked with an asterisk; and it shall be noted that the game was won by forfeit.

No contest is declared when a team does not appear due to inclement weather, an accident, vehicle break-

Scoring and Timing Regulations

Section 5	**Interrupted Games** When a game is interrupted because of events beyond the control of the responsible administrative authorities, it shall be continued from the point of interruption unless the teams agree otherwise or there are conference, league or association rules to cover the situation.
Section 6	**Protests** It is the policy of the NCAA Men's and Women's Basketball Rules Committees not to recognize or allow protests.
Section 7	**Length of Periods** Playing time shall be two halves of 20 minutes each with an intermission of 15 minutes between halves. Extra periods shall be five minutes each. *Note: By conference, league or association rules or by mutual agreement of both teams and the referee, the length of playing time periods for nonvarsity games may be reduced.*
Section 8	**Beginning and End of Period** Each period begins when the ball first becomes live. It ends when time expires except that:

down, illness or catastrophic causes. An institution shall not, for statistical purposes, declare a forfeit for nonfulfillment of a contract, but rather shall declare a "no contest."

a. If the ball is in flight during a try for field goal or in flight from a tap by a player toward his or her basket, the period ends when the try or tap ends.
b. If a held ball or violation occurs so near the expiration of time that the clock is not stopped before time expires, the period ends with the held ball or violation.
c. If a foul occurs so near the expiration of time that the timer cannot get the clock stopped before time

expires or if the foul occurs after time expires but while the ball is in flight during a try for field goal or in flight from a tap by a player toward his or her own basket, the period ends when the free throw or throws and all related activity have been completed. No penalty or part of a penalty carries over from one half or extra period to another.

> *Exception:* After the horn sounds to end the game, only those free throws necessary to determine the winner will be awarded.

d. If a technical foul occurs after the ball has become dead to end a period, the next period is started by administering the free throws. This applies when the foul occurs after the first and/or second half has ended, provided there is to be an extra period. If there is no way to determine whether there will be an extra period until the free throws are administered, the throws are attempted immediately, as if the foul had been part of the preceding period.

INTERPRETATIONS

Play 1: Time for the first half expires while the ball is in flight during a field-goal try by A1. B1 intentionally fouls A2 before the field-goal attempt has ended. After the ball has become dead after the last free throw by A2, A3 flagrantly fouls B1.
Ruling: A3 is disqualified. Because the foul by A3 was committed after the first half had expired, the second half will begin with the free-throw attempts by any Team B player(s). The foul by A3 is considered to have been made between the first and second halves.

Play 2: With a few seconds remaining on the game clock in the first half, A1 makes a throw-in to A2 (game clock not started—timer's error). A2 dribbles into the front court and misses the attempt. B1 recovers the rebound and dribbles the full length of the court. As the player passes the bench, the coach of Team A notices the game clock has not been started and calls the error to the timer's attention, who then starts the game clock. With one second left on the game clock in the half, A2 fouls B1. The bonus rule is in effect. Time expires before the timer can stop the game clock.
Ruling: Assess A2 with a personal foul. Administer the free throw(s) before the intermission. Referee may not correct this timer's error because the referee did not know exactly how much playing time was consumed while the game clock had been stopped.

Play 3: Team A is granted a timeout. The electric timer indicates no time remains in that period. However, the signal has not sounded.
Ruling: If the electric timer is working properly, the signal must sound to terminate the period.

Play 4: There are exactly eight seconds left on the game clock in the second half, and the ball is out of bounds in the possession of Team A. The throw-in by A1 touches the official on the court, and it goes across the court and out of bounds. The timer erroneously permits two seconds to run off the game clock.
Ruling: Either coach may step to the scoring table and request the timer to sound the sounding device because there has been a definite error made by the timer. The official should come to the sideline and confer with the coach or both coaches about the matter; and, if the official knows definitely that there were eight seconds

Timeout—Stopping Game and Shot Clocks

on the game clock when the ball was awarded to Team A for the throw-in, it is the responsibility of the official to put the two seconds time back on the game clock. If the official did not have definite information relative to when the ball was awarded for the throw-in and that the error was made, then the official shall not order the two seconds put back on the game clock. Neither coach would be penalized for drawing this matter to the attention of the official. (Rule 2-12)

Section 9 **Tie Score** If the score is tied at the end of the second half, play shall continue without change of baskets for one or more extra periods with a one-minute intermission before each extra period. The game ends if, at the end of any extra period, the score is not tied.

The length of each extra period shall be five minutes. As many such periods as are necessary to break the tie shall be played. Extra periods are an extension of the second half.

INTERPRETATION

Play: With the score tied, a foul is committed near the expiration of time in the second half. The free throw is successful.
Ruling: If the foul occurs before the ball becomes dead and the period is ended as outlined in Rule 5-8, no extra period is played. If the foul occurs after the period has clearly ended, the extra period begins with the free-throw attempt.

Section 10 **Timeout—Stopping Game and Shot Clocks** Timeout occurs and the game and shot clocks, if running, shall be stopped when an official:
a. Signals:
   (1) A foul.

Scoring and Timing Regulations

(2) A held ball.

(3) A violation.

b. Stops play:

(1) Because of an injury.

(2) To confer with scorers or timers.

(3) Because of unusual delay in a dead ball being made live.

(4) For any emergency.

Note 1: When a player is injured, the official may suspend play after the ball is dead or is in control of the injured player's team or when the opponents complete a play. A play is completed when a team loses immediate control (including throwing for goal) or withholds the ball from play by ceasing to attempt to score or advance the ball to a scoring position. When necessary to protect an injured player, the official may suspend play immediately.

Note 2: When a player incurs a wound that causes bleeding, the official must stop the game at the earliest possible time and instruct the player to leave the game for treatment by medical personnel. A player with blood on his or her uniform must have the uniform evaluated by medical personnel. If medical personnel determine that the blood has not saturated the uniform, the player may immediately resume play without leaving the game. If medical personnel rule that the blood has saturated the uniform, the affected part of the uniform must be changed before the player is allowed to return to the game.

c. Grants a player's visual or oral request for a time-out, such request being granted only when:

(1) The ball is in control or at the disposal of a player of his or her team. **Exception:** No timeout may be granted during an interrupted dribble.

(2) The ball is dead (after the throw-in starts, no

Timeout—Stopping Game and Shot Clocks

timeout may be granted to the opponents of the throw-in team).

(3) A disqualified or injured player(s) has been replaced when a substitute(s) is available.

d. (Women) Grants a coach's request for a timeout, such request being granted only when the coach's team is in possession of the ball (this includes throw-ins and free throws) or when the ball is dead. The official must be certain the request was made by a coach.

e. (Women) A coach or player on the court may request a timeout after a goal until a player on the team putting the ball in play from the end line is positioned out of bounds with the ball.

f. Responds to the scorer's signal to grant a coach's request that a correctable error as in Rule 2-10 or a timing, scoring or alternating-possession mistake be prevented or rectified. The appeal to the official shall be presented at the scorers' table where a coach of each team may be present.

Timeout occurs and the game clock, if running, shall be stopped after successful field goals in the last minute of the game and the last minute of any overtime period. Substitution is not allowed during this dead-ball situation.

INTERPRETATION

Play: While Team A is dribbling, the referee notices that there is blood on A1's jersey. The whistle is blown to stop play. A1 goes to the bench and medical personnel (a) determine that the jersey is not saturated with blood or (b) determine that the jersey is saturated with blood.

Ruling: In (a), player A1 may remain in the game without penalty. In (b), A1 must leave the game and

Scoring and Timing Regulations

change to a blood-free jersey. A1 must remain on the sideline until the next opportunity to substitute or Team A may use a timeout to allow A1 time to change the jersey. A1 may return to the game at the end of the timeout.

Section 11 **Charged Timeout** Timeout occurs and the game and shot clocks, if running, shall be stopped when:

a. (Men) A player requests a timeout, such request being granted only when the player's team is in possession of the ball (this includes throw-ins and free throws) or when the ball is dead.

b. (Women) A player or coach requests a timeout, such request being granted only when the player's/coach's team is in possession of the ball (this includes throw-ins and free throws) or when the ball is dead.

c. An injured player or a player who is bleeding or has a uniform that is saturated by blood elects to remain in the game.

> **(Men)** In games not involving commercial electronic media, each team is entitled to four full-length and two 20-second timeouts. The two 20-second timeouts may be used at any time during the game. A single charged timeout shall not exceed 75 seconds.
>
> In games involving commercial electronic media, when the commercial format calls for at least three timeouts in either half, each team is entitled to two full-length timeouts and three 20-second timeouts. Two of the three 20-second timeouts may be carried over from the first half to the second half.
>
> **(Women)** In games not involving commercial electronic media, each team is entitled to five full-length timeouts and one 20-second timeout per half. If a team has not used its 20-second timeout in the second half

> and the game goes into overtime, that 20-second timeout carries over to the extra period. No additional 20-second timeouts are allowed regardless of the number of overtime periods to be played. A single charged timeout shall not exceed 75 seconds.
>
> In games involving commercial electronic media, when the commercial format calls for at least three timeouts in either half, each team is entitled to three full-length timeouts and one 20-second timeout per half. If a team has not used its 20-second timeout in the second half and the game goes into overtime, that 20-second timeout carries over to the extra period. No additional 20-second timeouts are allowed regardless of the number of overtime periods to be played.

(**Men and Women**) Each team is entitled to one additional full-length timeout during each extra period. Unused full-length timeouts accumulate and may be used at any time. A signal, warning teams to prepare to resume play, is sounded 15 seconds before the expiration of the timeout. A signal shall then be sounded at the end of the timeout, and play shall resume immediately. Substitutions may not occur after the warning signal to prepare to resume play. A timeout shall be charged to a team for each 75 seconds or fraction thereof consumed under Rules 5-10-c, d and e regardless of the amount of time consumed.

Only one timeout is charged in Rule 5-10-b-(1) regardless of the amount of time consumed when an injured player remains in the game and in 5-10-f when no correction is made.

The team that calls the timeout may shorten the timeout if the captain tells the official of the team's intent.

In no case shall successive charged timeouts be granted after expiration of playing time for the second half or after the expiration of any overtime period. Successive timeouts may be taken if there is any time remaining to be played in any period.

Exceptions: No timeout is charged:
a. If in Rule 5-10-b-(1), an injured player is ready to play immediately or is replaced until at least the next opportunity to substitute after the clock has started after his or her replacement; or
b. If in Rule 5-10-c, the player's request results from displaced eyeglasses or lens; or
c. If in Rule 5-10-f, a correctable error, or a timing, scoring or alternating-possession mistake is prevented or rectified. If the time limit for correcting an error under Rule 2-10 has expired, a timeout is charged to the team making the appeal.

INTERPRETATIONS

Play 1: If an official on his or her own initiative takes a timeout to protect an injured player, should a timeout be charged to the team?
Ruling: After calling the timeout, the official should ask the player if the player desires a timeout. If the player does not, play should be resumed immediately. If the player is not ready to resume play immediately and is not replaced until at least the next opportunity to substitute after the clock has started, one timeout is charged to the injured player's team. Under no circumstances does the official have the authority to charge a timeout to himself or herself. [Rule 5-10-b-(1)]

Play 2: After the second half expires with the score tied, A1 is charged with a flagrant technical foul. Either Team A or B then requests and is granted a timeout. At the expiration of the timeout, B1 attempts the first free throw, which is either successful or unsuccessful. After the free throw, either Team A or B requests and is granted a timeout.

Ruling: Not legal. The second timeout is considered to be immediately after the first timeout.

Play 3: After the second horn sounds after a timeout, A1 goes to the free-throw line to attempt two free throws. (a) Before the first free throw, A6 reports to the scorer and tries to enter the game as a substitute or (b) after the first free throw is successful and before the ball is at the disposal of A1 for the second free throw attempt, A6 reports to the scorer and tries to enter as a substitute.

Ruling: In (a) A6 cannot enter the game because the second horn has sounded and there has been no live ball followed by a dead-ball sequence. In (b) A6 is allowed to enter because a live ball followed by a dead ball has occurred.

Section 12

Timeout—Starting Clock After time has been out, the clock shall be started when the official signals time in. If the official neglects to signal, the timer is authorized to start the clock unless an official specifically signals continued timeout.

a. If play is started by a jump ball, the clock shall be started when the tossed ball is legally tapped.

b. If a free throw is not successful and the ball is to remain live, the clock shall be started when the ball is touched by or touches a player on the court.

c. If play is resumed by a throw-in, the clock shall be started when the ball touches or is touched by a player on the court.

d. When play is resumed, the shot clock will start when team control is established.

Scoring and Timing Regulations

Section 13   **Excessive Timeout**   Timeouts in excess of the allotted number may be requested and shall be granted during regulation playing time or any overtime period at the expense of a technical foul for each.

Rule 6

Live Ball and Dead Ball

Rule 6

Live Ball and Dead Ball

Section 1 **Game—How Started** Unless a technical foul(s) has been called before the jump ball, the game and each overtime shall be started by a jump ball in the center circle. The second half starts with the team entitled to possession given the ball at the division line opposite the scorers' table. After any subsequent dead ball, the only way the ball may become live is to resume play by a jump ball, by a throw-in or by placing it at the disposal of a free thrower. The ball becomes live when:
a. On a jump ball, the ball leaves the official's hand.
b. On a throw-in, the ball is placed at the disposal of the inbounder.
c. On a free throw, the ball is placed at the disposal of the free thrower.

INTERPRETATION

Play: On a jump ball, the ball becomes live when it leaves the official's hand, but the clock does not start until the ball is tapped.
Ruling: Most jump-ball violations occur after the ball leaves the official's hand. If the ball did not become live until tapped, these would be acts during a dead ball and, therefore, different from most other violations. (Rules 5-12 and 9-7)

Section 2 **Center Jump—Alternating Process** Any two opponents may jump the ball at mid-court at the beginning of the game or extra periods. In jump-ball situations, other than at the start of the game and start of extra periods, teams will alternate taking the ball out of bounds at the spot nearest to where the jump-ball situation occurs.

The team that does not obtain control of the initial jump ball will start the alternating process by being awarded the ball out of bounds at the spot nearest to where the next jump-ball situation occurs.

INTERPRETATIONS

Play 1: Team A is entitled to a throw-in under the alternating process. Before the throw-in by Team A is completed, there is a foul called on either Team A or Team B.
Ruling: The procedure for any fouls called is not affected by the alternating process. The foul would be charged and penalized. Team A will make the throw-in when the next alternating process occurs. Team A did not lose its throw-in opportunity as a result of the foul.

Play 2: During the alternating process, Team A violates the throw-in provision by (a) leaving the designated throw-in spot, or (b) failing to pass the ball directly into the court so that after it crosses the boundary line it touches or is touched by another player (inbounds or out of bounds) on the court before it goes out of bounds, or (c) consuming more than five seconds before the ball is released, or (d) carrying the ball onto the court, or (e) touching it in the court before it has touched another player, or (f) throwing the ball so it enters the basket before touching anyone.
Ruling: When Team A violates the throw-in provision, it has lost its turn for a throw under the alternating process. Team B will make the next throw-in when an alternating process occurs.

Play 3: Team B is entitled to a throw-in under the alternating process. The official, or the scorer, makes an

Alternating-Possession Situations

error and the ball is erroneously awarded to Team A for the throw-in.

Ruling: Once the ball touches or is touched by an inbounds player, this situation cannot be corrected. However, Team B will make the throw-in when the next alternating process occurs. Team B did not lose its throw-in opportunity as a result of the error.

Play 4: The referee tosses the ball for the center jump to begin the game. Immediately after the ball is tapped by the jumpers, A2 and B2 tie the ball up.

Ruling: Since possession has never been established, the referee cannot use the alternating-possession arrow to award possession. In this case, the referee will toss the ball for another jump ball at the center circle. The players who tied the ball up will jump—in this case A2 and B2.

Play 5: During the opening jump ball, A1 illegally catches the tossed ball. The referee blows the whistle and awards the ball to B1 out of bounds at the division line. How is the alternating-possession arrow established?

Ruling: The first legal possession is by B1 on the throw-in. As soon as the throw-in by Team B ends, the alternating-possession arrow is changed toward Team A.

Section 3   **Alternating-Possession Situations**   The ball shall be put in play by the team entitled to the throw-in at the out-of-bounds spot nearest to where:

a. A held ball occurs.
b. The ball goes out of bounds as in Rule 7-3.
c. A double free-throw violation occurs.
d. A live ball lodges on a basket support. (*Exception*: During a throw-in, a live ball lodging on a basket support is a violation.)
e. The ball becomes dead when neither team is in control and no goal or infraction or end of a period is involved.

Live Ball and Dead Ball

f. After a double personal foul.

g. After simultaneous personal or technical fouls committed by the opponents.

The direction of the possession arrow is reversed immediately after an alternating-possession throw-in ends. An alternating-possession throw-in ends when the throw-in ends (Rule 4-34) or when the throw-in team violates the provisions of the throw-in.

The opportunity to make an alternating-possession throw-in is lost if the throw-in team violates the throw-in provisions. A foul by either team during an alternating-possession throw-in does not cause the throw-in team to lose the possession arrow.

Section 4 — Position for Jump Ball

a. For any jump ball, each jumper shall have both feet inside that half of the restraining circle that is farther from his or her own basket. The jumper may face in either direction. An official then shall toss the ball upward between the jumpers in a plane at right angles to the sidelines, to a height greater than either of them can jump and so that it will drop between them. The ball must be tapped by one or both of the jumpers after it reaches its highest point. If it touches the floor without being tapped by at least one of the jumpers, the official shall toss the ball again.

b. Neither jumper shall tap the tossed ball before it reaches its highest point, leave the jumping circle until the ball has been tapped, catch the jump ball, nor touch it more than twice. The jump ball and these restrictions end when the tapped ball touches one of the eight nonjumpers, the floor, the basket, the backboard or when the ball becomes dead.

c. When the official is ready to make the toss, a nonjumper shall not move onto the circle or change position around the circle until the ball has left the official's hand.

Resumption of Play by a Throw-in

d. None of the eight nonjumpers shall have either foot break the plane of the restraining circle cylinder nor may any player take a position in any occupied space until the ball has been touched. Teammates may not occupy adjacent positions around the restraining circle if an opponent indicates a desire for one of these positions before the official is ready to toss the ball. Players may move around the circle without breaking the plane of the cylinder after the ball has left the official's hand(s) during the toss.

INTERPRETATION

Play: During a jump ball, A1 touches the ball simultaneously with both hands and then again touches the ball simultaneously with both hands.
Ruling: If the jumper simultaneously touches the ball with both hands, that is considered touching the ball once; however, if one hand should touch slightly in advance of the second hand, that would be touching the ball twice.

Section 5 **Resumption of Play by a Throw-in** The ball shall be put in play by a throw-in under circumstances as outlined in Rules 7, 8-4 and 9-1 through 9-15.

INTERPRETATION

Play: After a timeout, Team A is entitled to the ball out of bounds. The referee blows the whistle indicating the timeout is over. When Team A is not at the inbounds spot ready to take the ball, the referee places the ball on the floor out of bounds at the disposal of Team A. The visible count begins and: (a) A1 picks up the ball and releases it for the throw-in within the allotted five seconds; (b) Team A does not pick up the ball

Live Ball and Dead Ball

within five seconds; (c) because Team A did not comply with throw-in provisions after a timeout, Team B is entitled to possession for a throw-in, but Team B does not get to the spot within five seconds after the referee places the ball on the floor at Team B's disposal.
Ruling: In (a), legal play. In (b), violation for Team A and the referee blows the whistle and begins a five-second count when the ball is handed to Team B for the in-bounds pass or placed on the floor at Team B's disposal. In (c), violation for Team B and the referee assesses a double technical foul. Each team is penalized for delay of game. No free throws are shot by either team and the ball is awarded by the alternating-possession arrow.

Section 6   **Ball at Disposal of Free Thrower** The ball shall be put in play by placing it at the disposal of a free thrower before each free throw.

Section 7   **Dead Ball** The ball becomes dead or remains dead when:

a. Any goal is made as in Rule 5-1.

b. It is apparent that the free throw will not be successful on a free throw for a technical foul or a false double foul or a free throw that is to be followed by another throw.

c. A held ball occurs or the ball lodges on the basket support.

d. An official's whistle is blown.

e. Time expires for a half or extra period.

f. A foul occurs.

g. Any floor violation (Rules 9-3 through 9-13) occurs, there is basket interference (Rule 9-15) or there is a free-throw violation by the thrower's team (Rule 9-1).

Dead Ball

Exception: The ball does not become dead until the try or tap ends when:

(1) d, e or f occurs while a try or tap for a field goal by a player toward his or her basket is in flight;

(2) d or f occurs while a try for a free throw is in flight;

(3) A foul is committed by an opponent of a player who has started a try or tap for goal (is in the act of shooting) before the foul occurred, provided time did not expire before the ball was in flight (The trying motion must be continuous and begins after the ball comes to rest in the player's hand or hands and is completed when the ball is clearly in flight. The trying motion may include arm, foot or body movements used by the player when throwing the ball at his or her basket. The tap starts when the player's hand(s) or finger(s) touch the ball in an attempt to tap it into his or her basket.); or (4) the ball is in flight on a try for field goal, a tap by a player toward his or her basket or during a free throw when an opponent swings his or her arm(s) or elbow(s) excessively without making contact. When the shooter, tapper, or his or her teammates commit this infraction, the ball becomes dead immediately.

INTERPRETATIONS

Play 1: The ball is in flight during a try or tap for field goal by A1 when time for a period expires. As time expires, the ball is on the ring or in the basket or is touching the cylinder above the basket when it is touched by: (a) A2; or (b) B1. The ball then goes through the basket or does not go through.
Ruling: In (a) or (b), the ball becomes dead when touched by anyone. However, if illegal touching is by

B1, two points are awarded to A1 (three points are awarded to A1 if it is a three-point try). Whether or not the ball goes through the basket has no effect upon the ruling. (Rules 4-36 and 9-15)

Play 2: As the hand of A1 contacts the ball to tap it toward the basket, B1 fouls A1. The ball is not airborne from the hand of A1.
Ruling: The penalty for a foul on a tap is the same as the penalty for a foul on a try. If the tap is successful, award one free throw. If the tap is unsuccessful, award two free throws.

Play 3: A1 rises and grabs the rebound clearly outside of the basket cylinder and, while airborne, stuffs the ball downward through the basket. Both hands are on the ball and in the basket when the electric horn sounds to signify the end of the period.
Ruling: This is ruled as no goal. Had the ball left the hands of A1 before the electric horn sounded to signify the end of the period, the dunk would have been the same as a try in flight; and the goal would have to be counted.

Rule 7

Out of Bounds and the Throw-in

Rule 7

Out of Bounds and the Throw-in

Section 1

Out of Bounds—Player, Ball A player is out of bounds when he or she touches the floor or any object other than a player on or outside a boundary. For location of a player in the air, see Rule 4-25.

The ball is out of bounds when it touches a player who is out of bounds; any other person, the floor, or any object on or outside a boundary; the supports or back of the backboard; or the ceiling, overhead equipment or supports. The ball is out of bounds if it passes over the backboard from any direction.

INTERPRETATIONS

Play 1: The ball rebounds from the edge of the backboard and across the boundary line; but before it touches the floor or any obstruction out of bounds, it is caught by a player who is inbounds.
Ruling: The ball is inbounds.

Play 2: The ball touches or rolls along the edge of the backboard without touching the supports.
Ruling: The ball is live unless ground rules to the contrary have been mutually agreed upon before the game.

Play 3: A1, while dribbling, touches: (a) B1 who is standing on a sideline or (b) a nearby chair or scorer's table while A1's feet are inbounds.
Ruling: (a) A1 is inbounds. However, if the ball in control of A1 touches B1, the ball is out of bounds and is awarded to Team A at that spot. (b) A1 is out of

Out of Bounds and the Throw-in

bounds because A1 touched an object that is out of bounds. Hence, the ball is considered to have gone out of bounds.

Play 4: Player A1 blocks a pass near the end line. The ball falls to the floor in bounds; but A1, who is off balance, is carried off the court. A1 returns, secures control of the ball, and dribbles.
Ruling: Legal. A1 has not left the court voluntarily and was not in control of the ball when leaving the court. This situation is similar to one in which A1 makes a try from under the basket and momentum carries A1 off the court. The try is unsuccessful, and A1 comes onto the court and regains control of the ball.

Section 2   **Ball Caused to Go Out of Bounds** The ball is caused to go out of bounds by the last player to touch or to be touched by it before it goes out, provided it is out of bounds because of touching something other than a player.

If the ball is out of bounds because of touching or being touched by a player who is on or outside a boundary, such player causes it to go out.

INTERPRETATIONS

Play 1: Ball passed by Team A touches an official and goes out of bounds.
Ruling: Team B's ball.

Play 2: A throw-in by A1 strikes B1 who is inbounds, rebounds from B1 directly into the air and then strikes A1 who is still out of bounds.
Ruling: A1 is considered to have caused the ball to go out of bounds, and it is awarded to Team B at that spot for a throw-in.

Out of Bounds, Ball in Play from

Section 3   **Ball Touched Simultaneously** If the ball goes out of bounds and was last touched simultaneously by two opponents, both of whom are inbounds or out of bounds, or if the official is in doubt as to who last touched the ball, or if the officials disagree, play shall be resumed by the team entitled to the alternating-possession throw-in at the spot out of bounds closest to where the simultaneous violation occurred.

Section 4   **Ball Awarded Out of Bounds** The ball is awarded out of bounds after:
    a. A violation as in Rule 9 or a double violation.
    b. A free throw for a technical foul as in Rule 8-4-b.
    c. A field goal or a successful free throw for personal foul as in Rule 8-4-a or an awarded goal as in Rule 9-15.
    d. The ball becomes dead while a team is in control provided no infraction or the end of a period is involved.
    e. A player-control foul.
    f. A common foul until the bonus rule goes into effect.
    g. A held ball as in Rule 4-21.

Section 5   **Out of Bounds, Ball in Play from**
    a. When the ball is out of bounds after any violation as outlined in Rules 9-3 through 15, the official shall hand the ball to or place the ball at the disposal of an opponent of the player who committed the violation for a throw-in from the designated spot nearest the violation. If the violation is on a throw-in, the new throw-in will be from the original spot.
    b. After a dead ball, as listed in Rule 7-4-d, any player of the team in control shall make the throw-in from the designated out-of-bounds spot nearest to the ball when it became dead.

c. After a player-control foul or after a common foul prior to the bonus rule being in effect, any player of the offended team shall make the throw-in from the designated spot nearest the foul.

d. If, in Rule 7-5-a, b or c, the throw-in spot is behind a backboard, the throw-in shall be made from the nearer free-throw lane line extended.

e. After a goal as listed in Rule 7-4-c, the team not credited with the score shall make the throw-in from the end of the court where the goal was made and from any point outside the end boundary line. Any player of the team may make a direct throw-in or may pass the ball along the end boundary line to a teammate behind the boundary line.

f. After a technical or intentional technical foul, any player of the team to whom the free throws have been awarded shall make the throw-in from out of bounds at the division line on either side of the court.

g. After a double personal foul, any player of the team to which the throw-in has been awarded under the alternating-possession procedure shall make the throw-in from the out-of-bounds spot nearest to where the foul occurred.

h. After a double technical foul, any player of the team to which the throw-in has been awarded under the alternating-possession procedure shall make the throw-in from out of bounds at the division line on either side of the court.

i. After a free-throw violation by the throwing team as listed in Rule 9-1, any opponent of the throwing team shall make the throw-in from out of bounds at the spot nearest to where the violation occurred.

j. After an intentional or flagrant personal foul, any player of the team to whom the throw-in has been awarded shall make the throw-in from the out-of-bounds spot nearest to where the foul occurred.

Out of Bounds, Ball in Play from

INTERPRETATIONS

Play 1: Team A scores a field goal. Team B requests and is granted a charged timeout.
Ruling: When the timeout is over, Team B may make the throw-in from anywhere behind the end line. Team B is not required to make the throw-in from a designated spot. The fact that Team B has taken a timeout does not restrict this privilege of throwing in from anywhere behind the end line. The same applies to a timeout after a successful free-throw attempt.

Play 2: When the official is required to hand the ball to the thrower-in, is it the duty of the official to wait until both teams are ready?
Ruling: No. The purpose of the rule requiring the official to hand the ball to the thrower-in other than after a timeout is to indicate clearly which team is entitled to the throw-in after the official has given the direction signal and other necessary information. Teams are expected to be ready for all normal play situations. If the official should inadvertently indicate the wrong team for a throw-in and then discover the error before play is resumed, the official should withhold the ball from play to permit the players to redeploy themselves. Officials should not permit unusual delays to allow a team to set up a scoring play in the front court or to permit a specific player to take the ball for a throw-in. (Rules 2-9-b and 10-2-a)

Play 3: (Men) A1 drives for a layup. After the ball leaves A1's hand but before it goes through the basket, A1 charges into B1. A1's try is successful. Team B is not in the bonus situation. The out-of-bounds spot nearest to where the foul occurred is on the end line. When the ball is handed to the thrower-in for Team B, may this player move along the end line?

Out of Bounds and the Throw-in

Ruling: In this situation, Team B is permitted to put the ball in play from any point out of bounds at the end line where the basket was scored. If it were ruled that the ball had to be put in play at the designated spot (point out of bounds nearest where the foul occurred), Team A would then be permitted to profit by committing the foul. The intent of the rules is to prohibit making it profitable to foul.

Section 6   **Throw-in** The throw-in starts when the ball is at the disposal of a player entitled to the throw-in. The throw-in count ends when the ball is released by the thrower-in so that it goes directly onto the court. The thrower-in shall release the ball within five seconds so that the pass goes directly into the court, except as provided in Rule 7-5-e. Until the passed ball has crossed the plane of the boundary: (1) the thrower shall not leave the designated throw-in spot (i.e., the thrower-in must have at least one foot on or over the designated spot). The thrower-in may jump vertically during the throw-in or move forward without stepping onto the court or move directly back from the boundary line as far as the player desires; (2) no opponent of the thrower-in shall have any part of his or her person over the inside plane of the boundary line; and (3) teammates shall not occupy adjacent parallel positions (shoulder to shoulder) near a boundary line if an opponent desires a spot between the positions. Teammates may occupy adjacent positions near a boundary line if the teammates take adjacent positions that are perpendicular to the boundary line (front to back single file).

INTERPRETATIONS

Play 1: Team A scores a field goal. B1 catches the ball as it goes toward the floor from the basket. B1 then steps out of bounds, runs a short distance and throws the ball to B2 who is standing out of bounds with one foot on but not beyond the end line. B2 does not break the plane of the inside edge of the end line until the ball has crossed the plane on the throw-in.
Ruling: Legal throw-in.

Play 2: A defensive player makes contact with the ball being passed between teammates out of bounds (Rule 7-5-e).
Ruling: The defensive player cannot interfere with the ball not yet inbounded. Technical foul.

Rule 8

Free Throw

Rule 8

Free Throw

Section 1 **Positions During Attempt** When a free throw is awarded, an official shall take the ball to the free-throw line of the offended team. After allowing reasonable time for players to take their positions, the official shall put the ball in play by placing it at the disposal of the free thrower. The same procedure shall be followed for each free throw of a multiple throw. During a free throw for a personal foul, each of the lane spaces adjacent to the end line shall be occupied by one opponent of the free thrower. A teammate of the free thrower is entitled to the next adjacent lane space on each side and to each other alternate position along each lane line. Only one player may occupy any part of a designated lane space and only the bottom lane space on each side must be occupied. If the ball is to become dead whether or not the last free throw for a specific penalty is successful, players shall not take positions along the free-throw lane. Only the four marked lane spaces on each lane line may be occupied. All other players must be behind the free-throw line extended and behind the three-point field-goal line.

Note: To avoid disconcerting the free thrower, no official should stand in the free-throw lane or the lane extended.

INTERPRETATION

Play: During the first of two free-throw attempts by A1, B2 does not occupy third lane space and A3 takes it. Before the ball is handed to A1 for the second try, B2 requests permission to occupy the third space.
Ruling: Grant request of B2.

Free Throw

Section 2 **Who Attempts**

a. Personal fouls—The free throw or throws awarded because of a personal foul shall be attempted by the offended player. If such player must withdraw because of an injury, because the player is bleeding or has blood on the uniform or because of disqualification, the player's substitute shall attempt the throw or throws unless no substitute is available, in which event any teammate may attempt the throw or throws.

b. Technical fouls—The free throw awarded because of a technical foul may be attempted by any player, including an entering substitute, of the offended team. The captain shall designate the free thrower for a technical foul (see Rule 3-4).

INTERPRETATIONS

Play 1: A2 attempts a free throw that should have been taken by A1.
Ruling: If the attempt by A2 is due to a justifiable misunderstanding, there is no penalty. The error may be corrected under Rule 2-10. If it is reasonable to believe that A2 knew that A1 was the designated shooter, a technical foul for unsporting conduct shall be called. The technical foul will be administered after A1 shoots the free throw to which he or she is entitled.

Play 2: A1 is fouled by B1 and appears injured as a result. The official suspends play at the proper time. Team A indicates it desires a timeout. At the expiration of the timeout, it is apparent that a substitute for A1 is not necessary. Before the signal is given to resume play, A6 reports and is beckoned onto the court by an official. A6 indicates he or she is to replace A1, which would avoid a timeout being charged to Team A.
Ruling: A1 is required to attempt the free throw or throws unless an injury prevents A1 from doing so.

Ball in Play if Free Throw is Missed

Section 3   **10-Second Limit**   The try for goal shall be made within 10 seconds after the ball has been placed at the disposal of the free thrower at the free-throw line. This shall apply to each free throw.

Section 4   **Next Play**   After a free throw that is not followed by another free throw, the ball shall be put in play by a throw-in:

a. As after a field goal (Rule 7-4) if the try is successful and is for a personal foul, other than an intentional or flagrant foul;

b. By any player of the free thrower's team from out of bounds at the division line if the free throw is for a technical foul; or

c. By any player of the free thrower's team from the out-of-bounds spot nearest the foul for any flagrant personal foul or any intentional foul.

Section 5   **Ball in Play if Free Throw is Missed**   If a free throw for a personal foul is unsuccessful, or if there is a multiple throw for a personal foul (or fouls) and the last free throw is unsuccessful, the ball remains live.

If there is a multiple throw and both a personal and technical foul are involved, the tries shall be attempted in the order in which the related fouls were called; and if the last try is for a technical or flagrant personal foul, the ball shall be put in play at the division line or the spot nearest to where the foul occurred, respectively.

INTERPRETATION

Play: Team A is assessed a technical foul. Right after the ball is handed to B1 at the free-throw line by the official, A2 pushes B2 flagrantly. Referee disqualifies A2 from the contest.

Free Throw

Ruling: No players will take positions along the free-throw lane for B1's two free-throw attempts or for B2's two free-throw attempts. After B2's two free throws, Team B will be awarded the ball for a throw-in at the spot nearest to where the flagrant personal foul was committed.

Section 6 **Ball in Play After False Double Foul** After the last free throw following a false double foul (Rule 4-14-h), the ball shall be put in play as if the penalty for the last foul of the false double foul were the only one administered. When the last foul is a double personal foul, the ball will be awarded to the team entitled to the alternating-possession throw-in.

Rule 9

Violations and Penalties

Free Throw

Rule 9

Violations and Penalties

Section 1   **Free Throw** A player shall not violate the following free-throw provisions:

a. The try shall be attempted from within the free-throw semicircle and behind the free-throw line.

b. After the ball is placed at the disposal of a free thrower:

  (1) The free thrower shall throw within 10 seconds and in such a way that the ball enters the basket or touches the ring before the free throw ends.

  (2) The free thrower shall not purposely fake a try nor shall the free thrower's teammates or opponents purposely fake a violation.

  (3) No opponent shall disconcert the free thrower.

  (4) No player shall enter or leave a marked lane space.

  (5) The free thrower may not break the vertical plane of the free-throw line with either foot until the ball strikes the ring or backboard, or until the free throw ends. The free thrower shall not enter or leave the semicircle.

  (6) Players not in a marked lane space must be behind the free-throw line extended and behind the three-point field-goal line until the ball strikes the ring or backboard, or until the free throw ends.

  (7) Players occupying any of the four marked lane spaces on each side of the lane may break the vertical plane of a lane-space boundary once the free thrower has released the ball.

c. An opponent of the free thrower shall occupy each lane space adjacent to the end line during the try, and no teammate of the free thrower may occupy either of these lane spaces.

INTERPRETATIONS

Play 1: A1, at the free-throw line to attempt a free throw, is handed the ball by the official, who starts a silent count. A1 strikes his or her knee or leg accidentally with the ball while bouncing it. It rolls toward the basket between the free-throw-lane lines.
Ruling: It is customary in such instances for the official to sound the whistle at once, causing the ball to become dead immediately. The official should caution the free thrower, place the ball at the disposal of A1 and start a new silent count.

Play 2: Before a free throw is released, a player in the second lane space extends arms over the area between the lane spaces.
Ruling: Legal if there is no contact.

Play 3: The ball is at the disposal of free thrower A1. B1, within the visual field of A1: (a) raises the arms above the head, or (b) after the arms have been extended above the head, alternately opens and closes both hands.
Ruling: If the official judges the act in either (a) or (b) to be disconcerting, the official is obligated to penalize it. The burden not to disconcert is that of the free thrower's opponents.

Play 4: Before a free throw by A1 is in flight: (a) A2 pushes B2, and then A3 steps into the free-throw lane too soon; or (b) A3 steps into the free-throw lane too soon, and then A2 pushes B2. The bonus rule is in effect for both teams.

Free-Throw Violation Penalties

Ruling: In (a), the foul by A2 causes the ball to become dead immediately. A3 did not commit a violation because the ball became dead when A2 fouled. A1 now attempts the free throw with no players on the lane. The foul by A2 is then penalized, creating a false-double-foul situation. After the one-and-one attempts by B2, play is resumed as though the last foul of the false double foul was the only one administered. In (b), the ball becomes dead when A3 violates the free-throw lane provisions; therefore, the pushing of B2 by A2 is ignored unless it was flagrant, unsporting or intentional. (Rule 4-14)

Play 5: On a free-throw attempt by A1, B1 commits a lane violation. A1's free throw subsequently misses the ring.
Ruling: Double violation; alternating possession rule is invoked.

Section 2   **Free-Throw Violation Penalties**
a. If a violation is by the free thrower or the free thrower's teammate only, no point can be scored by that throw. The ball becomes dead when the violation occurs. For any violation or personal (common, intentional or flagrant) foul, the ball is awarded out of bounds at the spot nearest to where the violation or personal foul occurred.
b. If a violation is by the free thrower's opponent only: if the try is successful, the goal counts and the violation is disregarded; if it is not successful, the ball becomes dead when the free throw ends and a substitute throw shall be attempted by the same thrower under the same conditions as the original throw.
c. If there is a violation by each team, the ball becomes dead when the violation by the free thrower's team occurs, no point can be scored, and play shall be

Violations and Penalties

resumed by awarding the ball out of bounds to the team entitled to the throw-in at the spot nearest to where the double violation occurred.

d. The out-of-bounds provision in Rule 9-2-a and the alternating-possession provision in Rule 9-2-c do not apply if the free throw is to be followed by another free throw or if there are free throws by both teams. In Rule 9-2-c, if a violation by the free thrower follows disconcertion, a substitute free throw shall be awarded.

INTERPRETATION

Play: A2 and B2 commit lane violations (double violation) during (a) the first free throw of a one-and-one bonus by A1 or (b) the first of two free-throw attempts by A1 or (c) the last or only free throw.

Ruling: In (a) or (c) the free throw is canceled and the alternating possession rule applies. In (b) the first free throw is canceled and the second free throw is administered normally.

Section 3   **Ball Out of Bounds** A player shall not cause the ball to go out of bounds.

Section 4   **Throw-in** A player shall not violate provisions governing the throw-in. The thrower-in shall not:

a. Leave the designated throw-in spot.

b. Fail to pass the ball directly into the court so that after it crosses the boundary line, it touches or is touched by another player (inbounds or out of bounds) on the court before going out of bounds. A throw-in that lodges on the rim is a violation.

c. Consume more than five seconds from the time the throw-in starts until the ball is released.

d. Carry or hand the ball onto the court.

e. Touch it in the court before it has touched another player.

f. Throw the ball so that it enters the basket before touching anyone, strikes the back of the backboard or supports, passes over the backboard, or bounces into the court from a balcony or from the floor out of bounds. No player shall:

g. Become the thrower-in or be out of bounds after a designated spot throw-in begins.

h. Be out of bounds when he or she touches or is touched by the ball after it has crossed the vertical inside plane of the boundary line.

i. The opponents of the thrower-in shall not have any part of their person beyond the vertical inside plane at any end line or sideline before the ball has crossed the line.

INTERPRETATIONS

Play 1: Thrower-in A1 attempts deception by throwing the ball against the edge of the front face of the backboard, after which it caroms into the hands of A2. **Ruling:** The edge and front face of the backboard are inbounds and, in this specific circumstance, are treated the same as a floor inbounds. Hence, the throw-in is legal.

Play 2: During a throw-in by Team A, A1's (a) foot breaks the plane of the boundary line or (b) A1's hand(s) and the ball break the plane of the boundary line. **Ruling:** No violation in either (a) or (b).

Section 5 **Travel, Kick or Fist** A player shall not travel or run with the ball, kick it, strike it with the fist or cause it to enter and pass through the basket from below. Kicking the ball is striking it intentionally with the knee, any

Violations and Penalties

part of the leg below the knee or the foot.
Note: Kicking the ball is a violation only when it is a positive act; accidentally striking the ball with the foot or leg is not a violation.

Section 6   **Double Dribble** A player shall not dribble a second time after the player's first dribble has ended, unless it is after the player has lost control because of:
a. A try for field goal.
b. A bat by an opponent.
c. A pass or fumble that has then touched or been touched by another player.

Section 7   **Jump Ball** A player shall not violate any provision of Rule 6-4. If both teams simultaneously commit violations during the jump ball, or if the official makes a bad toss, the toss shall be repeated.

Section 8   **Three-Second Rule** A player shall not remain for three seconds in that part of the player's free-throw lane between the end boundary and the farther edge of the free-throw line while the ball is in control of the player's team in his or her front court. Allowance shall be made for a player who, having been in the restricted area for less than three seconds, dribbles or moves in to try for goal. If the player passes the ball instead of trying for goal, the player will be called for a violation. The count shall not begin or it shall be terminated during an interrupted dribble. All lines designating the free-throw lane are part of the lane, and touching these lines constitutes being in the lane.

INTERPRETATION

Play: The ball is loose.
Ruling: The three-second count is in effect unless it is during an interrupted dribble. The team that had

Shot Clock

control before the loose ball maintains team control until the opponent secures control.

Section 9 **10-Second Rule** (Men) A player shall not be (and his team shall not be) in continuous control of a ball that is in his backcourt for 10 consecutive seconds.

INTERPRETATION

Play: (Men) A1 is in the backcourt and has dribbled for eight seconds when he passes the ball forward toward A2 in the front court. While the ball is in the air, traveling from backcourt to front court, the 10-second count expires.

Ruling: Violation. Award the ball to Team B out of bounds at the spot nearest to where A1 was standing when he threw the ball.

Section 10 **Shot Clock** The team in control shall attempt a try for field goal within 35 seconds for men and within 30 seconds for women after gaining team control. The try shall leave the shooter's hand before the expiration of the allotted shot-clock time, and the try subsequently shall strike the basket ring or enter the basket.

INTERPRETATIONS

Play 1: Just after the shot-clock signal is sounded, the ball is shot by a player on the free-throw line.

Ruling: The ball should be put in play closest to the position of the ball at the time the shot-clock period elapsed, in this case, at the end line.

Play 2: B1 blocks A1's try for goal and the shot clock expires. The shot-clock horn sounds (a) while the ball is loose on the court, or (b) while A2 gains possession of

Violations and Penalties

the ball, or (c) while the blocked try is in the air and the ball subsequently strikes the basket ring or goes in the basket, or (d) while B2 has gained possession of the ball. **Ruling:** In (a) and (b), Team A has committed a shot-clock violation because the try did not strike the basket ring. In (c), the shot-clock horn is ignored and play continues with a shot-clock reset upon possession by either team because A1 complied with the shot-clock rule when the try struck the basket ring or entered the basket. In (d), the shot-clock horn is ignored and play continues with Team B getting a shot-clock reset.

Play 3: A1 releases the ball on a try for goal. After the ball leaves A1's hand, the shot-clock horn sounds. The ball (a) hits the backboard and then goes through the net; (b) hits the backboard and rebounds directly to A2 or B1 without hitting the rim; or (c) hits the backboard, strikes the basket ring and rebounds directly to A2. **Ruling:** In (a), score the field goal. In (b), a shot-clock violation by Team A has occurred because the try did not hit the rim. The referee sounds the whistle, and the ball is awarded out of bounds to Team B at the spot nearest the violation. In (c), there is no shot-clock violation because the try hit the rim. The shot clock is reset when Team A establishes possession of the ball on the rebound.

Play 4: With the alternating possession arrow favoring Team A and 12 seconds remaining on the shot clock, A1's try for goal has left A1's hand and subsequently is legally blocked by B1 and does not strike the basket. The ball (a) is recovered by A2 or (b) goes out of bounds or (c) is simultaneously recovered by A3 and B3 and the official rules a held ball or (d) is possessed by A4 who subsequently is tied up by B4 and the official rules a held ball.

Basketball

Ball in Backcourt

Ruling: In (a), (b) and (d), the shot clock is not reset and Team A has 12 seconds in which to comply with the shot clock rule. In (c), because team control ended when A1's try for goal left the hand and no player on Team A regained control before the held ball occurred, the shot clock should be reset with Team A being awarded a throw-in out of bounds closest to the spot of the held ball.

Play 5: With the alternating possession arrow favoring Team A and 20 seconds remaining on the shot clock, A1's try for goal lodges in between the backboard and basket support.
Ruling: Team A gets possession for a throw-in with the shot clock being reset.

Section 11 **Ball in Backcourt** A player may not be the first to touch the ball in his or her backcourt if the ball came from the front court while the player's team was in team control and the player or a teammate caused the ball to go to the backcourt. A player causes the ball to go to the backcourt by having the ball touch any part of his or her body voluntarily or involuntarily. A pass in the front court that is deflected by a defensive player so that the ball goes into the backcourt may be recovered by either team.

Exception 1: It is not a violation when, after a jump ball or during a throw-in, a player is the first to secure control of the ball while both feet are off the floor and the player then returns to the floor with one or both feet in the backcourt.

Exception 2: It is not a violation when a defensive player secures control of the ball while both feet are off the floor and the player then returns to the floor with one or both feet in the backcourt.

INTERPRETATIONS

Play 1: A1 receives a pass in Team A's front court and throws the ball to his or her backcourt where the ball (a) is touched by a teammate, (b) goes directly out of bounds or (c) lies or bounces with all players hesitating to touch it.

Ruling: Violation when touched in (a). In (b), it is a violation for going out of bounds. In (c), the ball is live so that B may secure control. If A touches the ball first, it is a violation. The ball continues to be in team control of A. For men, the 10-second count starts when the ball arrives in the backcourt while the 35-second shot clock continues to run. For women, the 30-second clock also continues to run.

Play 2: B1 (a) secures possession of a rebound from Team A's basket or (b) has the ball for a throw-in under Team A's basket. B1 is in the front court of Team A (in other words, the backcourt of Team B). B1 attempts a long pass down the court to teammate B2. A2, standing in Team A's front court close to the division line, leaps high in the air and intercepts a pass by B1 and then returns to the court, in the backcourt of Team A, with the ball in control.

Ruling: In (a) and (b), no violation has occurred as these two situations are exceptions to the backcourt rule (see Rules 4-25 and 9-11).

Section 12   **Elbow(s)** A player shall not excessively swing his or her arm(s) or elbow(s), even though there is no contact with an opponent. Obviously, a player may extend arm(s) or elbow(s) to hold the ball under the chin or against the body. Action of arm(s) and elbow(s) resulting from total body movement as in pivoting or movement of the ball incidental to feinting with or releasing it or moving it to prevent a held ball or loss of control is not considered excessive.

The official will, however, consider it to be excessive swinging if:

(1) arm(s) and elbow(s) are swung about while using the shoulders as pivots, and the speed of the extended arm(s) and elbow(s) is in excess of the rest of the body as it rotates on the hips or on the pivot foot; or

(2) the speed and vigor with which the arm(s) and elbow(s) are swung is such that injury could result if another player were contacted.

INTERPRETATION

Play: While A1's try for a field goal is in flight or A1's tap is in flight toward Team A's basket, B1 violently swings arm(s) and elbow(s) and makes no contact with any Team A player.

Ruling: The official shall sound the whistle immediately; however, the ball does not become dead until it is apparent the tap or try is made or missed. If the try or tip is successful, the basket counts and the violation is ignored. If the tap or try is unsuccessful, Team A is awarded the ball at the out-of-bounds spot nearest to where B1 violated. If a teammate of A1 committed a violation as B1 did, the ball would be dead immediately and no points could be scored. The ball would be awarded to Team B out of bounds at the spot nearest to where the violation occurred.

Section 13   **Closely Guarded** Closely guarded situations occur when:
a. A team in its front court controls the ball for five seconds in an area enclosed by screening teammates.
b. A player in control of the ball, but not dribbling, is

Violations and Penalties

closely guarded when an opponent is in a guarding stance within six feet. A closely guarded violation occurs when the player in control of the ball holds the ball for more than five seconds (for men, in the front court only).

INTERPRETATION

Play: Team A, while in possession of the ball, lines up four of its players side by side, just inbounds at a boundary line. The four players pass the ball back and forth to one another with their arms reaching out beyond the plane of the boundary line. The players are in (a) the front court or (b) the backcourt.
Ruling: In (a), at the end of five seconds, a violation is called. In (b), the 10-second rule applies for men.

Section 14 **Floor-Violation Penalties (Applies to Rules 9-3 through 9-13)** The ball becomes dead or remains dead when a violation occurs. The ball is awarded to a nearby opponent for a throw-in at the out-of-bounds spot nearest the violation. If the ball passes through a basket during the dead-ball period immediately after a violation, no point(s) can be scored and the ball is awarded to an opponent out of bounds at the spot nearest to where the violation occurred.

Section 15 **Basket Interference and Goaltending**
a. A player shall not touch the ball or basket when the ball is on or within either basket. The ball is considered to be within the basket when any part of the ball is below the level of the ring.
b. A player shall not touch the ball when it is touching the cylinder, which has the ring as its lower base.
c. A player shall not touch the ball outside the cylinder while reaching through the basket from below.

Basket Interference and Goaltending

d. A player shall not touch the ball during a field-goal try while it is in its downward flight entirely above the basket-ring level and has the possibility of entering the basket in flight or touch the ball outside the cylinder during a free-throw attempt.

e. A player shall not touch a ball that has been tapped by a player toward his or her basket while the ball is in its downward flight entirely above the basket-ring level and has the possibility of entering the basket in flight.

Exception: In Rules 9-15-a or b, if a player has a hand legally in contact with the ball, it is not a violation if this contact with the ball continues after it enters a basket cylinder or if, in such action, the player touches the basket.

INTERPRETATIONS

Play 1: The ball is touching the side of the basket ring of Team A. B1 jumps and contacts the net. The ball definitely is not touching the top of the basket ring.
Ruling: This is not a violation. Ball remains live.

Play 2: B1 touches the ball while a throw-in is in the cylinder above the basket or the ball is on the basket ring.
Ruling: Basket interference. Team A is awarded two points. Team B is awarded the ball for a throw-in, as after a scored goal, except that the official shall hand the ball to a player of Team B and the player or a teammate shall make the throw-in. (Rule 7-5-a)

Play 3: While the ball is touching the top of the ring of the basket on a field-goal attempt, a player grasps the ring.
Ruling: This is a double infraction. It is both basket interference and a technical foul. The moment the hand touched the ring, it was basket interference.

Violations and Penalties

When the player grasped the ring, a technical foul occurred. (Rule 10-3-f)

Play 4: The ball enters the basket during a field-goal try by A1. Before the ball is in flight for the try, A1 is fouled. A2 touches the rim while the ball is in the basket.
Ruling: A2 commits basket interference and the goal is canceled. Award A1 two free throws because of the foul.

Play 5: A1 rebounds the ball while part of the ball is in the basket cylinder and, in the same continual motion, dunks the ball.
Ruling: Basket interference. The ball becomes dead when A1 contacts the ball in the basket cylinder, and the dunking or stuffing of the dead ball is ignored. The basket is disallowed.

Play 6: A1 throws the ball down into the basket from above and from outside of the imaginary cylinder. A1's hand loses contact with the ball before the ball enters the cylinder. However, on the follow-through the hand enters the cylinder and again contacts the ball.
Ruling: It is a violation when a player touches the ball while any portion of the ball is touching the imaginary cylinder directly above the basket and the player did not carry the ball into cylinder or basket.

Play 7: A1 attempts a two-point try and while the ball is in the air, time expires. (a) While the ball is on its way to the basket, B1 legally touches it and subsequently the ball enters the basket or (b) B1 legally touches it and subsequently B2 commits a goaltending violation.
Ruling: In (a) and (b) the goal shall count and two points are awarded to A1.

Play 8: The ball is in flight during a three-point

Basket Interference and Goaltending Penalties

field-goal try by A1 when time for a period expires. After the expiration of time and while the ball is rolling on the ring, B1 taps it into the basket.
Ruling: Basket interference by B1. Three points are awarded to A1 because of the interference.

Play 9: The bonus rule is in effect. While the ball is in flight during a try for a three-point field goal, A1 charges into B1. B2 then commits a basket-interference violation.
Ruling: Both the violation and the personal foul are penalized. Team A is awarded three points for the basket interference by B2, and then B1 is awarded a free throw (or throws) for the charging foul by A1. (Men) If the foul by A1 is Team A's seventh, eighth or ninth foul, award a one-and-one opportunity. If A1's foul was the 10th foul or more for that half, award two free throws.

Section 16 **Basket Interference and Goaltending Penalties** If the violation is at the basket of the opponent of the offending player, the offended team is awarded:

a. One point for basket interference or one point and a technical foul for goaltending if during a free throw.
b. Two points if during a two-point field goal.
c. Three points if during a three-point field goal.

The crediting of the score and subsequent procedure is the same as if the awarded score had resulted from the ball having gone through the basket, except that the official shall hand the ball to a player of the team entitled to the throw-in.

If the violation is at a team's own basket, no points can be scored and the ball is awarded to the offended team at the out-of-bounds spot nearest to where the violation occurred.

Violations and Penalties

If the violation results from touching the ball while it is in the basket after entering from below, no points are scored and the ball is awarded out of bounds to the opponent at the spot nearest to where the violation occurred.

If there is a violation by both teams, play shall be resumed by awarding the ball to the team entitled to the alternating-possession throw-in at the out-of-bounds spot nearest to where the simultaneous violations occurred.

Rule 10

Fouls and Penalties

Rule 10

Foulsand Penalties

Technical Fouls

Section 1 **Forfeiture** The referee may forfeit a game if any player, squad member or bench personnel fails to comply with any technical foul, makes a travesty of the game or when any conditions warrant a forfeiture. The referee shall forfeit the game if a team refuses to play after being instructed to do so by an official. The official has the authority to determine the length of time that may elapse before the forfeit is declared. Conference policy may include an established time limit.

Section 2 **Administrative Procedures** The following six situations are cause for a technical foul to be charged to a team, or in the case of substitution, to a player:

a. Delay of game. A team shall not delay the game. This includes when the clock is not running, consuming a full minute through not being ready when it is time to start either half; failure to supply scorers with data as outlined in Rule 3-3; delaying the game by preventing the ball from being promptly put in play. This includes but is not exclusive to delaying the administration of a throw-in or free throw by engaging in a team huddle any place on the court. Chairs/stools must be removed immediately after the first horn of any timeout and clean-up must be completed before the final horn signalling the resumption of play. One warning will be given to a team that fails to do this; a technical foul will be assessed thereafter.

b. Starting lineup/squad list. A team shall not change its designated starting lineup or add to its squad list

Fouls and Penalties

(see Rules 3-3-a and b).

c. Number of participants. A team shall not have more than five squad members participating simultaneously.

d. Excessive timeouts. A team shall not be granted excessive timeouts without penalty.

e. Substitution. A substitute shall not enter the court without reporting to scorers, without the substitute's name appearing on the pregame squad list or without being beckoned onto the court by an official (unless between halves).

f. Musical Instruments. The playing of musical instruments while the game is in progress is not permitted.

Note: Substitutions between halves shall be made to the scorer before the signal that ends the intermission.

PENALTY: The penalty for administrative technical fouls is two free throws and possession of the ball to the offended team. None of the administrative technical fouls count toward a player's five fouls for disqualification or toward the team foul total.

For (b) and (c), an infraction shall be penalized if it is discovered during the time the rule is being violated.

INTERPRETATIONS

Play 1: After a field goal by B1, the score is A-61, B-60. A1 has the ball out of bounds for a throw-in with four seconds remaining in the game. A1 holds the ball. (a) B2 crosses the boundary line and holds A1 or (b) B2 reaches through the out-of-bounds plane and slaps the ball from the hands of A1 or touches the ball as it is passed along the end line after a score. Time expires close to the moment the official indicates the infraction. **Ruling:** In (a), an intentional personal foul is charged to B2. In (b), an intentional technical foul (two shots) is charged to B2. The time remaining to play is in no way a factor. The circumstances do not permit a warning. If A1, making the throw-in, reaches through the out-of-bounds plane into the court and B1 then slaps the ball from the hands of A1, without B1 breaking the plane above the out-of-bounds line, the ball becomes live and B1 has not committed a violation.

Play 2: Team A has a player who is assessed a fifth personal foul and therefore disqualified from the game. The referee notifies the player, the coach and the timer, who then starts the 30-second time period. When the buzzer sounds, the coach of Team A has not replaced the disqualified player.
Ruling: Team A is assessed a technical foul for delay of game. Allow the substitute to legally enter the game and resume play with a player from Team B shooting two free throws, followed by possession to Team B at the division line. This is a technical foul assessed to the head coach and one of three toward disqualification.

Play 3: Team A is not ready to take the court after the second horn sounds to indicate the end of the half-time intermission.
Ruling: The referee should ask the timer to start the device used to time timeouts. At the expiration of one minute, Team A is assessed a technical foul for delay of game. Team B shoots two free throws and gets possession of the ball at the division line. If Team A was entitled to the possession arrow, it does not lose the arrow in this situation. This technical foul is administrative in nature and is not charged to the head coach or toward the team's bonus situation.

Section 3	**Conduct of Players** A player shall not engage in the following conduct without being charged a noncontact technical foul:

Fouls and Penalties

a. Participate after changing his or her number without reporting it to the scorers and an official.

b. Participate after having been disqualified.

c. Wear an identical number (this item also applies to all squad members included in the list of names supplied to the scorers, Rule 3-3).

d. Wear an illegal number.

e. Wear an illegal shirt.

f. Grasp either basket during the time of the officials' jurisdiction. **Exception:** A player may grasp the basket if, in the judgment of an official, the player is trying to prevent an obvious injury to himself or herself or another player.

g. (Men) Dunk or stuff or attempt to dunk or stuff a dead ball before or during the game or during any intermission until jurisdiction of the officials has ended (this item applies to all squad members).

h. Slap or strike the backboard or cause either the backboard or ring to vibrate while the ball is in flight during a try or tap, is touching the backboard, is on or in the basket or in the cylinder above the basket. A player may not place a hand(s) on the backboard to gain an advantage.

i. Leave the court for an unauthorized reason.

INTERPRETATIONS

Play 1: Team A sets up a double screen for A1, who in attempting to come across the free-throw lane is legally obstructed by offensive and defensive players so that A1 leaves the court under the basket, out of bounds, circles around, returns to the court and then receives the ball. **Ruling:** Technical foul is charged to A1 for leaving the court for an unauthorized reason. Whether A1 receives the ball has no bearing on the decision.

Play 2: A player steps out of bounds to avoid contact. **Ruling:** This is not a foul unless the player leaves to deceive in some way. If the player is a dribbler, the ball is out of bounds.

j. Purposely delay his or her return to the court after being legally out of bounds.
k. Attempt to gain an advantage by interfering with the ball after a goal, by failing to immediately pass the ball to the nearer official if in control when a violation is called, or by repeated infractions of Rules 9-4-h and 9-4-i.
l. Delay the game by preventing the ball from being promptly made live.
m. Touch a ball in flight during a free-throw attempt.

PENALTY: The penalty for technical fouls involving conduct of players is two free throws and possession of the ball to the offended team. *Exception:* **In the instance that double technical fouls are committed, no free throws are awarded and the ball is awarded by the alternating possession arrow.**

None of the technical fouls mentioned above count toward a player's five fouls for disqualification or toward a team's bonus free-throw situation.

For (a) and (b), a technical foul shall be assessed and the offender shall be disqualified. For (d) and (e), an infraction shall be penalized if discovered before the ball becomes live.

A player who receives a combination of three technical fouls or two unsporting conduct technical fouls is ejected and must go to the team's locker room until the game is over.

Fouls and Penalties

INTERPRETATIONS

Play 1: (Men) Fifteen minutes before the game is scheduled to start, and during the warm-up, squad member A6 dunks and is charged with the infraction. In defiance, A6 dunks a second time and a third time.
Ruling: Team B is awarded six free throws, and A6 is disqualified from participation in the game.

Play 2: A1 dunks and in so doing grasps the ring: (a) before the ball leaves his or her hand; or (b) after the ball clears the net.
Ruling: In (a), for men, A1 is assessed with two technical fouls, one for grasping the ring and the other for dunking a dead ball. For women, A1 is assessed a technical foul for grasping the ring. In (a), no goal is scored. In (b), the goal is counted and A1 is assessed a technical foul for grasping the ring.

Play 3: A1 is dribbling toward the basket and contact is made by B1 immediately before the start of the act of dunking. A1 continues the attempt to stuff or dunk the ball.
Ruling: If the official sounds the whistle and calls a foul on either A1 or B1, the basket does not count. For men, A1 is not assessed a technical foul for dunking a dead ball, as long as the official believes there was reasonable doubt that A1 heard the whistle or that he could not react quickly enough to stop the dunk.

Play 4: A1 is in the act of dunking the ball, and a foul is called on B2 or B1 off the ball.
Ruling: If A1 has started the throwing motion, the goal counts. For men, no foul is called on A1 for dunking in this situation. If the foul off the ball is committed before A1 starts his throwing motion, the official still does not call a technical foul on A1 for dunking a

Unsporting Conduct of Players

dead ball if there is reasonable doubt that A1 heard the whistle. The referee does not count the basket and penalizes for the foul that was committed off the ball. (Rule 10-3-f)

Section 4 **Unsporting Conduct of Players** To be unsporting is to act in a manner unbecoming a fair, ethical, honorable individual. A player shall not use unsporting tactics without being charged a noncontact technical foul. Unsporting tactics include, but are not limited to, the following:

a. Disrespectfully addressing or contacting an official or gesturing in such a manner as to indicate resentment.
b. Using profanity or vulgarity; taunting, baiting or ridiculing another player; or pointing a finger at or making obscene gestures toward another player.
c. Purposely obstructing an opponent's vision by waving hands near his or her eyes.
d. Climbing on or lifting a teammate to secure greater height.
e. Knowingly attempting a free throw to which he or she is not entitled.
f. Accepting a foul that should be charged to a teammate.
g. Faking being fouled.
h. Inciting undesirable crowd reaction.
i. Intentionally or flagrantly contacting an opponent when the ball is dead.
j. Using smokeless tobacco.

PENALTY: The penalty for noncontact technical fouls involving unsporting conduct of players is two free throws and possession of the ball to the offended team.

Exception: **In the instance that double technical fouls are committed, no free throws are awarded and the ball is awarded by the alternating possession arrow.**

Fouls and Penalties

The unsporting, noncontact technical fouls mentioned above count toward a player's five fouls for disqualification and toward the team foul total. Two unsporting technical fouls assessed to a squad member shall be considered a flagrant technical foul and lead to ejection.

All personnel ejected from the game must go to the locker room until the game is over.

Section 5 Unsporting Conduct of Bench Personnel (Coaches, Substitutes, Team Attendants) and Followers

Any bench personnel, including coaches, substitutes and team attendants, and any fans of a team shall be assessed a technical foul for the following unsporting conduct:

a. Disrespectfully addressing an official.
b. Attempting to influence an official's decision.
c. Using profanity or language that is abusive, vulgar or obscene.
d. Taunting or baiting an opponent.
e. Objecting to an official's decision by rising from the bench or using gestures.
f. Inciting undesirable crowd reactions.
g. Entering the court unless by permission of an official to attend an injured player (see exceptions under bench-area restrictions).
h. Failing to replace a disqualified or injured player within 30 seconds if a substitute is available.
i. Using smokeless tobacco.
j. Using electronic transmission (i.e., headsets) to and from the bench area and using television monitoring or replay equipment at court side for coaching purposes.
k. Refusing to occupy the team bench to which a team was assigned.
l. Purposely throwing debris onto the court once the officials' jurisdiction has begun.

Unsporting Conduct of Bench Personnel and Followers

PENALTY: The penalty for technical fouls involving unsporting conduct of bench personnel and followers is two free throws and possession of the ball to the offended team. *Exception:* In the instance that double technical fouls are committed, no free throws are awarded and the ball is awarded by the alternating possession arrow.

The bench technical fouls mentioned above count toward a substitute's five fouls for disqualification (even though the player is not participating in the game at that moment) and the team foul total.

All of the unsporting technical fouls mentioned above are assessed to the offender, are charged to the head coach or cohead coaches and count toward the team foul total. Two unsporting technical fouls assessed directly to bench personnel lead to ejection. The head coach or cohead coaches shall be ejected after two technical fouls have been assessed directly to him or her or after three bench technical fouls have been called on his or her team (e.g., technical fouls assessed to a team manager, a trainer and a substitute also are assessed to the head coach and lead to ejection).

All personnel ejected from the game must go to the team's locker room until the game is over.

An assistant coach who replaces the ejected head coach does not inherit any technical fouls the head coach may have had. However, the assistant is responsible for technical fouls previously assessed to him or her in that game.

Fouls and Penalties

INTERPRETATIONS

Play 1: A1 is driving toward the basket when the official, while trailing the play and advancing in the direction in which the ball is being advanced, is sworn at by the coach of the opposing team.
Ruling: The official shall withhold the whistle until A1 has either made or missed the layup. The official then shall sound the whistle and assess the coach a technical foul, which could be flagrant.

Play 2: The official is advancing up court to cover the play and, as the official passes the bench with his or her back to it, someone on Team A's bench uses uncomplimentary language. The official is certain from which bench it came but not from which party.
Ruling: When the official cannot, with assurance, determine the violator, the official shall charge the technical foul to the head coach. The official alone shall decide to whom a technical foul is to be charged. It is not the prerogative of the coach or someone on the bench to come forward as the party guilty of poor bench decorum.

Play 3: The referee notices that the head coach of Team A is using a headset to communicate with someone in the stands. This is discovered (a) before the start of the game or (b) during the game.
Ruling: In (a), the official asks the coach to remove the headset and discontinue using it. In (b), a technical foul is assessed.

Play 4: Player A4 is disqualified from the game after receiving his or her fifth foul. The coach of Team A does not have a substitute ready to enter the game after the 30-second substitution clock expires.

Bench-Area Restrictions

Ruling: The referee blows the whistle and calls a technical foul on Team A. This technical foul is assessed to the coach and is one of the three the head coach can accrue before being ejected from the game. Team A's substitute must enter the game. Team B shoots two free throws and gets possession of the ball at the division line.

Section 6   **Flagrant Technical Fouls** A flagrant technical foul is a noncontact foul that involves extreme, sometimes persistent, vulgar, abusive conduct such as described in Rules 10-4 and 10-5.

PENALTY: The penalty for a flagrant technical foul is two free throws and possession of the ball to the offended team. The offender is automatically ejected from the game and must go to the team's locker room until the game is over.

Exception: In the instance that double flagrant fouls are committed, no free throws are awarded, the offenders are automatically ejected from the game, and the ball is awarded by the alternating possession arrow.

Section 7   **Bench-Area Restrictions** All bench personnel except the head coach shall remain seated on the bench while the clock is running and the ball is live except to spontaneously react to an outstanding play, immediately sitting down afterward. A head coach may leave his or her place on the bench, but in doing so, shall stay within the confines of his or her team's coaching box.

Bench personnel are allowed to leave the confines of the bench area only under the following circumstances:
a. A coach or team attendant may leave the confines of the coaching-box area to seek information from the

scorer or timer during a timeout or intermission.
b. A squad member may leave the bench area to report to the scorers' table.
c. A coach, squad member or team attendant may leave the confines of the bench at any time to point out a scorers' or timers' mistake, or to request a timeout for a correctable error (Rule 2-10). If there was no mistake on the part of the scorer or timer, or the error is not correctable under Rule 2-10, a timeout shall be charged to the offending team.
d. The head coach may leave the confines of the bench area if a fight may break out or has broken out on the court. Any bench personnel other than the head coach who leave the confines of the bench area during a fight that may break out or has broken out shall be disqualified from participating in the game and shall go to the team's locker room until the game has ended. No technical fouls are assessed.
e. During an intermission or a timeout charged to a team, the coach and/or team attendants may confer with their players at or near the bench as long as it is done within the confines of the bench area.

In all other circumstances, bench personnel must remain in the coaching-box area. No part of a foot may touch or be beyond the outer edge of the boundaries of the coaching box.

INTERPRETATION

Play: A team has coheads coaches.
Ruling: Before the start of the game, the team must designate who the coach with "standing" privileges will be for the entire game. Both coaches will be assessed all bench technical fouls.

Fighting

Section 8 **Fighting** Fighting, as defined in Rule 4-13, includes, but is not exclusive to:

a. An attempt to strike an opponent with the arms, hands, legs or feet.

b. An attempt to punch or kick an opponent, regardless of whether contact is made.

c. An attempt to instigate a fight by committing an unsporting act toward an opponent that causes the opponent to retaliate by fighting.

As determined by the officials, fighting is a flagrant foul and can be either personal (while the ball is live) or technical (during a dead ball).

PENALTY: For any flagrant technical or personal foul committed by a coach, squad member, team attendant or follower, two free throws shall be awarded and the offender shall be ejected and go to the team's locker room until the game is over.

Exception: In the instance that double flagrant fouls are committed, no free throws are awarded, the offenders are automatically ejected from the game, and the ball is awarded by the alternating possession arrow.

For any technical foul, the ball will be awarded to the offended team at the division line for a throw-in. For any flagrant personal foul, the ball will be awarded to the offended team at the designated spot nearest the foul.

Any squad member, coach or other team personnel who participates in a fight (regardless of whether he or she is an active player at the time) shall be assessed a flagrant foul. The first time that individual participates in a fight during the season (including exhibition games), the individual will be suspended from participating in the team's next regular season game (not an exhibition contest), including tournament competition. If the same individual participates in a second fight, that individual will be suspended for the remainder of the season, including tournament competition. If an individual participates in a fight during his or her team's final game of the season, that individual will be suspended from participating in the team's next regular-season game for which that player, coach or other team personnel would be eligible. Any player, coach or other team personnel under suspension for fighting may not sit on the team bench. (See page 164 for a summary of fight reporting procedures.)

The referee may forfeit the game if any individual fails to comply with any part of the above penalties.

INTERPRETATIONS

Play 1: The head coach of Team A is standing within the coaching box to coach his or her team. Likewise, two assistant coaches and 10 squad members are standing while the clock is running and the ball is live. Is this legal?
Ruling: If only one other person is illegally standing, assess both the individual and the head coach a technical foul. If more than one other person is standing, assess a technical foul to only the head coach.

Play 2: A6 and B6 leave the bench because a fight has broken out. A6 and B6 do not participate in the fight.
Ruling: A6 and B6 are ejected from the game. No free-throw penalties or technical fouls are assessed to A6 and B6. Both A6 and B6 must go to the locker room until the game has ended.

Play 3 A6 and A7 leave the bench because a fight has broken out. A6 and A7 participate in the fight.

Ruling: A6 and A7 are ejected from the game immediately upon leaving the bench and entering the court. Flagrant technical fouls are assessed to A6 and A7 for fighting. These technical fouls also are assessed to the head coach because A6 and A7 are regarded as bench personnel. A6 and A7 also are assessed the proper penalty under the fighting-suspension rule. For the first fight, A6 and A7 shall be suspended for the next and immediate game. For the second fighting offense by A6 and A7, they shall be suspended for the balance of the season, including tournament competition. If these players fought during the final game of the season, they will be suspended from participation in the team's next regular-season game for which they would be eligible. They may not sit on the team bench while under suspension for fighting.

Personal Fouls

Section 9   **Types** A player shall not hold, push, charge or trip; nor impede the progress of an opponent by extended arm, shoulder, hip or knee or by bending the body into other than a normal position; nor use any rough tactics. A player shall not contact an opponent with his or her hand unless such contact is only with the opponent's hand while it is on the ball and is incidental to an attempt to play the ball. The use of hands on an opponent in any way that inhibits the freedom of movement of the opponent or acts as an aid to a player in starting or stopping is not legal. Extending the arms fully or partially other than vertically so that freedom of movement of an opponent is hindered when contact with the arms occurs is not legal. These positions are employed when rebounding, screening or engaging in various aspects of post play. A player may not use the forearm and hand to prevent an opponent from attacking the ball during a dribble or when throwing for goal. A player may hold the hands and arms in front of his or her face or body for protection and to absorb force from an imminent charge by an opponent. Contact caused by a defensive player approaching the ball holder from behind is a form of pushing, and that, caused by the momentum of a player who has thrown for goal, is a form of charging.

INTERPRETATIONS

Play 1: B1 takes a certain spot on the floor before A1 jumps from the floor to catch a pass. (a) A1 returns to the floor and lands on B1, or (b) B1 moves to a new spot while A1 is airborne. A1 comes to the floor on one foot and then charges into B1.
Ruling: In both (a) and (b), the foul is on A1.

Play 2: (Men) The bonus is in effect; and, while the ball is in flight during a try for a field goal, A1 charges into B1 which is Team A's seventh foul in the half. After this, there is a basket-interference violation by: (a) B2, or (b) A2.
Ruling: (a) Both the foul by A1 and the violation by B2 are penalized, but in the reverse order of occurrence. First, two points are awarded to Team A because of the violation by B2; B1 then is awarded a one-and-one, and the ball shall remain live if the last throw is not successful and it touches the basket ring. If A1's foul was Team A's 10th foul or more, including any combination of personal, unsporting and contact technical fouls, award two shots; and the ball remains in play. Beginning with the 10th foul, including any

combination of personal, unsporting and contact technical fouls, in a half, two shots are awarded for each common foul (except player control). In (b), there are no rule complications. The violation caused the ball to become dead. Ordinarily, the ball would go to Team B out of bounds at the spot closest to the violation. However, this penalty is ignored because of the penalty enforcement for the foul by A1. Had the bonus rule not been in effect, the ball would have been awarded out of bounds to Team B at the spot closest to the foul. (Rule 9-15)

Play 3: A1 is running toward Team A's goal but is looking back to receive a fast break outlet pass. B1 takes a position in the path of A1 while A1 is 10 feet away from B1. (a) A1 runs into B1 before receiving the ball; or (b) A1 receives the ball and, before taking a step, contacts B1.
Ruling: In both (a) and (b), A1 is responsible for contact. B1 took a position in the path of A1 that was far enough away from A1 to avoid contact.

Play 4: While in the act of shooting a three-point field-goal try, A1 is fouled by B1. The ball: (a) enters the basket or (b) does not enter the basket. In both (a) and (b), A2 commits basket interference at Team A's basket.
Ruling: In both (a) and (b), the goal does not count and A1 is awarded three free throws. (Rule 9-15)

Play 5: (Men) B1 is standing behind the backboard before A1 jumps for a layup shot. The forward momentum of A1 causes a charge into B1.
Ruling: B1 is entitled to the position provided there was no movement into such position by B1 after A1 leaped from the floor. If the ball goes through the basket before the contact occurs, the contact is ignored

Fouls and Penalties

unless B1 has been placed at a disadvantage by being unable to rebound if the shot is missed or unable to put the ball in play without delay, if the try was successful. If the contact occurs before the ball becomes dead, a charging foul has been committed by A1. If B1 moves into the path of A1 after A1 has left the floor, the foul is on B1. It is always an intentional foul when a player moves into the path of an airborne opponent with the intent to undercut and contact results. If the moving player moves under the airborne opponent and there is danger of severe injury as a result of the contact, it is a flagrant foul.

Play 6: (Women) B1 is standing behind the plane of the backboard before A1 jumps for a layup shot. The forward momentum of airborne shooter A1 causes a charge into B1.

Ruling: B1 is entitled to the position provided there was no movement into that position after A1 left the floor. If the ball goes through the basket before or after the contact occurs, it is a player-control foul and the goal is canceled. If B1 moves into the path of A1 after A1 has left the floor, the foul is on B1. It is a two-shot blocking foul when the defensive player moves into the path of the airborne shooter with no intent to play the ball. If the defensive player moves under the airborne shooter and does not play the ball but rather takes away the landing spot, it is a two-shot blocking foul. If a defensive player is trying to establish legal defensive position and makes a legitimate attempt to play the ball, it does not automatically constitute a two-shot foul.

Section 10 **By Dribbler** A dribbler shall not charge into nor contact an opponent in the dribbler's path nor attempt to dribble between two opponents or between an opponent and a boundary, unless the space is such as to provide a reasonable chance for the player to go through without contact. If a dribbler, without contact, passes an opponent sufficiently to have head and shoulders past the front of the opponent's torso, the greater responsibility for subsequent contact is on the opponent. If a dribbler in his or her progress has established a straight-line path, the dribbler may not be crowded out of that path; but, if an opponent is able to legally establish a defensive position in that path, the dribbler must avoid contact by changing direction or ending the dribble. The dribbler should not be permitted additional rights in executing a jump try for goal, pivot, feint or the start of a dribble.

Section 11   **By Screener**   A player who screens shall not:

a. When outside the visual field of a stationary opponent, take a position closer than a normal step from the opponent.

b. When assuming a position at the side or in front of a stationary opponent, make contact with that opponent. If the screen is set within the visual field of a stationary opponent, the screener may be as close to the opponent as the screener desires, short of contact.

c. Take a position so close to a moving opponent that this opponent cannot avoid contact by stopping or changing direction.

d. After assuming a legal screening position, move to maintain it, unless the screener moves in the same direction and path of the opponent. When both opponents are moving in exactly the same path and same direction, the player behind is responsible if contact is made because the player in front slows up or stops and the player behind overruns his or her opponent.

In (c), the speed of the player to be screened will determine where the screener may take a stationary position. This position will vary and may be one to two normal steps or strides from the opponent.

It is legal for screeners to line up parallel and next to each other as long as the screen is set at least six feet from a boundary.

If the screener violates any of these provisions and contact results, the screener has committed a personal foul.

A player who is screened within his or her visual field is expected to avoid contact by going around the screener. In cases of blind screens, the opponent may make inadvertent contact with the screener; and, if the opponent is running rapidly, the contact may be severe. Such a case is to be ruled as incidental contact provided the opponent stops (or attempts to stop) on contact and moves around the screen, and provided the screener is not displaced if he or she has the ball. A player may not use the arms, hands, hips or shoulders to force his or her way through a screen or to hold the screener and then push the screener aside in order to maintain a guarding position relative to his or her opponent.

INTERPRETATION

Play: A defensive player maneuvers to a position in front of the pivot player A1 to prevent A1 from receiving the ball. A high pass is made over the head and out of reach of the defensive player. The pivot player A1 moves toward the basket to catch the pass and try for goal. As the pass is made, a teammate of the defensive player moves into the path of A1, in a guarding position.
Ruling: This action involves a screening principle. The defensive player has switched to guard a player who does not have the ball. Therefore, the switching player must assume a position one or two strides in advance of

the pivot player (depending upon the speed of movement of the pivot player) to make the action legal. If A1 has control of the ball (provided the pivot player is not in the air at the time), the play becomes a guarding situation. If it is a guarding situation involving the player with the ball, time and distance are irrelevant.

Section 12 **Personal-Foul Penalties** The offender is charged with one foul, and if it is the offender's fifth foul, including any combination of personal, unsporting and contact technical fouls, or if it is flagrant, the offender is disqualified.

The offended player is awarded free throws as follows:
a. One free throw for:
   (1) A foul against a player who attempts a field goal and whose try or tap is successful.
   (2) Each nonflagrant foul that is a part of a multiple foul and is not a player-control foul, regardless of whether the offended team is in the bonus.
b. Two free throws for:
   (1) A foul against a player who attempts a field goal and whose try or tap is unsuccessful.
   (2) An intentional personal or flagrant personal foul and the ball awarded out of bounds to the offended team at the spot nearest to where the intentional or flagrant personal foul occurred.
   (3) Any single flagrant foul and the ball awarded out of bounds to the offended team at either end of the division line. Flagrant personal fouls result in ejection from the game for the offender.
   (4) (Women) A blocking foul against the airborne shooter if the basket is missed.
   (5) (Men) Each common foul (except player control), beginning with a team's 10th foul that

results from a combination of personal, unsporting and contact technical fouls during the half.

(6) Each flagrant foul of a multiple foul and the ball awarded out of bounds to the offended team.

(7) A multiple foul (unless the offended player attempted a three-point field goal that was unsuccessful) if either foul is intentional or flagrant and the ball awarded out of bounds to the offended team.

c. Three free throws for:

A foul against a player who attempts a three-point field goal and whose try or tap is unsuccessful. If the foul is intentional or flagrant, the ball also is awarded out of bounds to the offended team at the spot nearest to where the foul occurred.

d. Bonus free throw for:

Each common foul (except player-control) beginning with a team's seventh personal, unsporting or contact technical foul during the half, provided the first attempt is successful.

e. No free throws for:

(1) Each common foul before the bonus rule is in effect.

(2) A player-control foul.

(3) A double foul, even if one or both of the fouls are flagrant or intentional.

f. In case of a false double foul or a false multiple foul, each foul carries its own penalty.

Personal-foul penalty exception: After the horn sounds to end the game, only those free throws necessary to determine a winner will be awarded.

INTERPRETATIONS

Play 1: A guard moves into the path of a dribbler and contact occurs.
Ruling: Either player may be responsible, but the greater responsibility is that of the dribbler if the guard conforms to the following principles that officials use in reaching a decision. The guard is assumed to have established a guarding position if the guard is in the dribbler's path facing him or her. If the guard jumps into position, both feet must return to the floor after the jump, before he or she has established a guarding position. No specific stance or distance is required. It is assumed the guard may shift to maintain his or her position in the path of the dribbler provided the guard does not charge into the dribbler nor otherwise cause contact as outlined in Rule 10-10. The responsibility of the dribbler for contact is not shifted merely because the guard turns or ducks to absorb shock when contact caused by the dribbler is imminent. The guard may not cause contact by moving under or in front of a passer or thrower after the passer or thrower is in the air with his or her feet off the floor.

Play 2: One or both fouls of either a multiple foul or a double foul is flagrant.
Ruling: For a multiple foul, one free throw is awarded for each nonflagrant foul and two free throws for the flagrant foul. For a double personal foul, no free throws are awarded. In either case, any player who commits a flagrant foul is disqualified.

Play 3: The score is tied when the referee calls a shooting foul on Team B as (a) the horn sounds simultaneously to end the game or (b) four seconds remain on the game clock.

Fouls and Penalties

Ruling: In (a), award two free throws to A1. If A1 makes the first shot, the game is over. In (b), A1 is awarded two free throws. If A1 makes both free throws, Team B is awarded the ball out of bounds on the baseline under Team A's basket.

Play 4: Team A is winning 79-70 when a foul is called against Team B as (a) the horn sounds simultaneously to end the game or (b) five seconds remain on the game clock.

Ruling: In (a), no free throws are awarded because a winner already has been determined—in this case Team A. In (b), the free throws are awarded because time remains on the clock.

Summary—Administration of Double Fouls

Foul	Penalty	Resumption of Play
Double personal foul	No shots	Alternating-possession arrow
Double flagrant (live ball)	No shots, ejection	Alternating-possession arrow
Double technical (dead ball)	No shots	Alternating-possession arrow
Double flagrant technical	No shots	Alternating-possession arrow

Fight Reporting Procedures

1. The referee informs the player, the head coach and the scorer that an ejection for fighting was issued (the scorer notes in the score book).

2. After the game, the referee contacts the supervisor of officials/ assigner for the game and reports player

ejection(s).

3. The supervisor of officials/assigner reports the ejection(s) to the conference commissioner.

4. The conference commissioner contacts by phone and follows up in writing to the following people:

   a. The athletics director of the team whose player(s) was involved and

   b. If the opponent player(s) was ejected, that team's conference commissioner or, if an independent institution, that team's athletics director.

5. Player ejection procedures should be handled quickly since the eligibility of the player(s) is impacted with a second fight.

6. Related considerations:

   a. The head coach should withhold the player from the next scheduled game even if the conference or athletics director has not contacted him or her.

   b. Institutional and conference policy dictates if a suspended player is permitted to attend the game from which he or she is suspended. If the player(s) attends the game, he or she is not allowed to sit on the team bench.

Officiating Guidelines

Coach and Bench Decorum

Coaches and/or other bench personnel who engage in the following actions are in violation of the bench decorum rules and should be assessed a technical foul:

a. Questioning the integrity of an official by words or gestures.

b. Physically charging toward an official.

c. Directing personal, vulgar or profane remarks or

Fouls and Penalties

gestures toward an official.

d. Excessively demonstrating officiating signals (e.g., traveling, holding, verticality) or excessively demonstrating by use of gestures or actions that indicate displeasure with officiating. If not excessive, a warning should be given to keep it from becoming excessive.

e. Voicing displeasure about officiating through continuous verbal remarks. A warning could be given initially to keep it from becoming continuous.

f. Using disrespectful or unsporting words, gestures or actions toward an opposing player or coach.

g. Leaving the coaching box for an unauthorized reason.

Post Play

Some guidelines to officials in making correct, consistent calls in low-post play:

a. Observe the entire play, especially when responsible for off-ball coverage.

b. Anticipate the play but not the call when post players are in fronting situations.

c. When the defensive player pushes a leg or knee into the rear of the offensive player, it is a foul on the defender.

d. When the offensive player dislodges a defensive player from an established position by pushing or backing in, it is a foul on the offensive player.

e. If a player uses the "swim stroke" arm movement to lower the arm of an opponent, it is a foul.

f. If either post player uses hands, forearms or elbows to prevent an opponent from maintaining a legal position, it is a foul.

Hand Checking (Impeding the Progress of a Player)

To curtail hand checking, officials must address it at the beginning of the game, and fouls must be called consistently throughout the game. Some guidelines for officials to use when officiating hand checking:

a. When a defensive player keeps a hand or forearm on an opponent, it is a foul.

b. When a defensive player puts two hands on an opponent, it is a foul.

c. When a player continually jabs by extending his or her arms and placing a hand or forearm on the opponent, it is a foul.

Screening

Officials responsible for coverage away from the ball must be diligent in detecting and penalizing illegal screens. Some guidelines for officials to use when officiating screening situations:

a. When a player uses arms, hands, hips or shoulders to force through a screen or to hold or push the screener, it is a foul.

b. When contact results because a player sets a screen while moving, the screener commits a foul.

c. When a screener takes a position so close to a moving opponent that this opponent cannot avoid contact by stopping or changing direction, it is a foul.

d. When a player sets a screen outside the visual field of a stationary opponent and does not allow this opponent a normal step to move, it is a foul.

Hanging on the Rim

It has become obvious during the past several seasons that players are hanging on the basket ring in an excessive, emphatic manner during dunk shots when there is no evidence of an injury occurring. The intent of the rule does not provide for a player to hold the ring and lift his body or legs, or in general, hang on the rim for emphasis. This is especially true for a player who dunks the ball on a breakaway or when no defender is nearby. Injuries, sometimes serious, occur as a result of hanging on the rim. Game delays also result when damaged equipment must be fixed or replaced. When there is no obvious injury circumstance involved, hanging on the rim is a technical foul and must be called.

Intentional Fouling

Guidelines that might be helpful in calling the intentional foul are:

a. Any foul that is not a legitimate attempt to directly play the ball or a player is intentional.

b. Running into the back of a player who has the ball, wrapping the arms around a player or grabbing a player around the hips are definitely intentional fouls.

c. Grabbing a player's arm or body while initially attempting to gain control by playing the ball directly is intentional.

d. Grabbing, holding or pushing a player away from the ball is intentional.

e. Undue roughness to stop the clock is an intentional foul and if severe should be called flagrant.

f. It is an intentional foul if, while playing the ball, a player causes excessive contact with an opponent.

The intentional foul must be called within the spirit and intent of the intentional-foul rule.

Official Signals

Official Basketball Signals

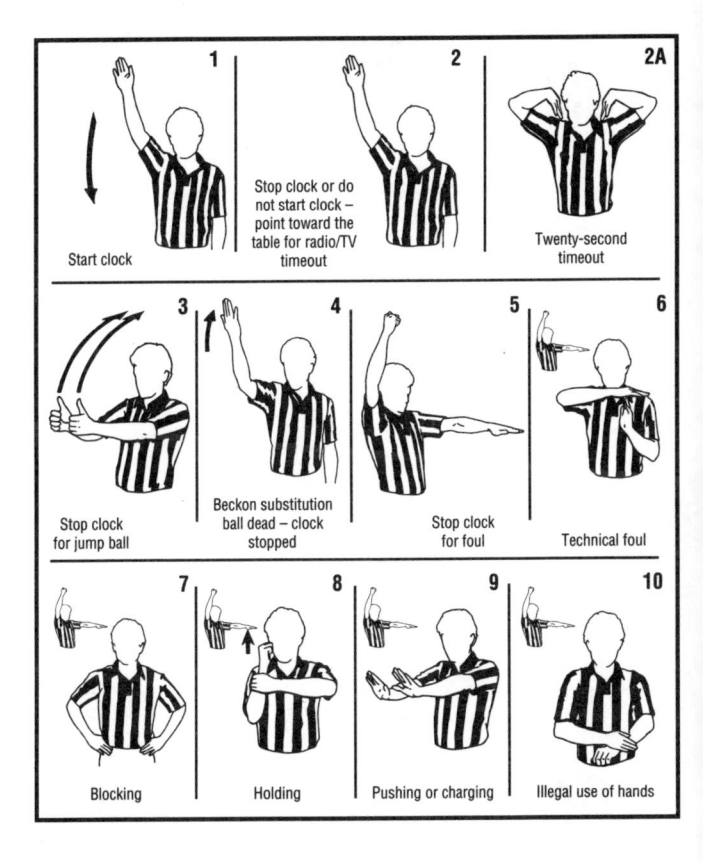

1	Start clock
2	Stop clock or do not start clock – point toward the table for radio/TV timeout
2A	Twenty-second timeout
3	Stop clock for jump ball
4	Beckon substitution ball dead – clock stopped
5	Stop clock for foul
6	Technical foul
7	Blocking
8	Holding
9	Pushing or charging
10	Illegal use of hands

The number assigned to each signal corresponds with numbering in the Collegiate Commissioners Association officiating manuals.

Official Rules

Official Signals

12A Intentional foul

12B Double foul

12C Intentional foul/Excessive contact

11 Player control foul

13 Traveling

14 Illegal dribble

15 3 second violation

16 Over and back or carrying the ball

17 Throw-in, free throw or designated spot violation

18 5 or 10 second violation – use both hands for 10

19 Directional signal — AND / PLUS*

20 Designates out-of-bounds spot

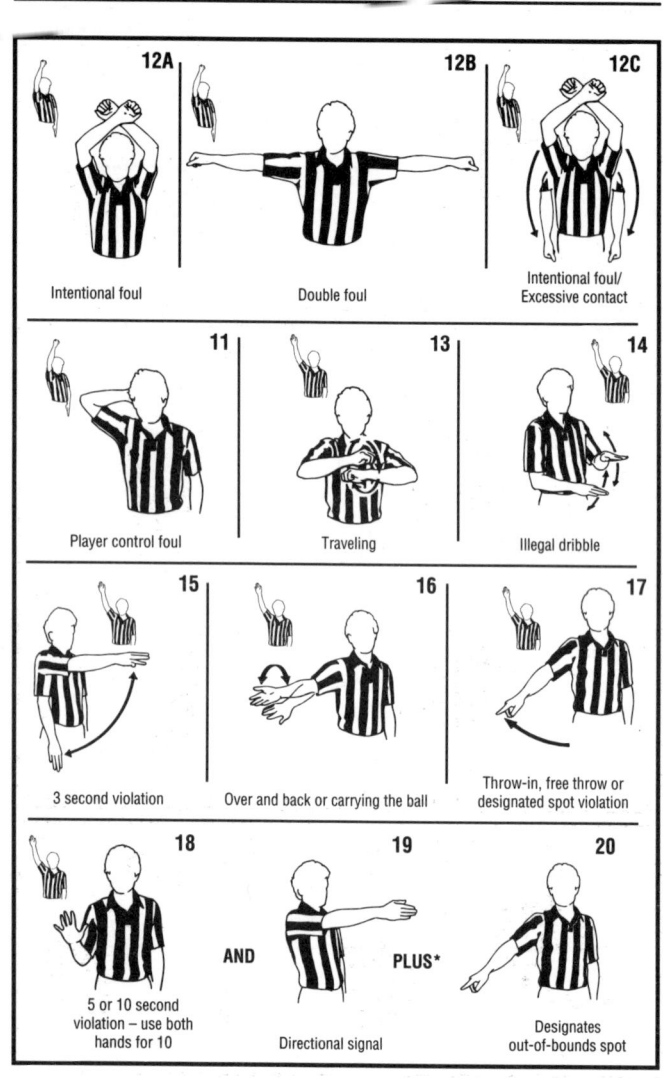

172 Basketball

Official Signals

24 Bonus free throw
for 2nd throw drop 1 arm –
for 2 throws use 1 arm with 2 fingers –
for 3 throws use 1 arm with 3 fingers

26 3-point field goal — Attempt — and if successful

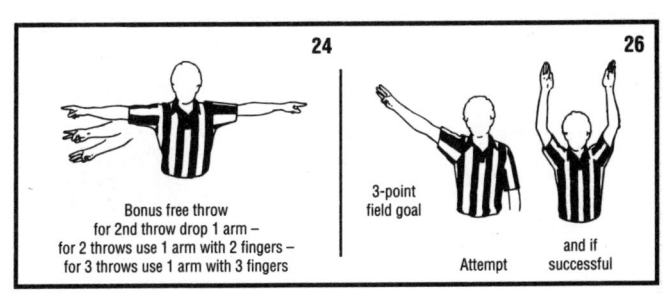

21 No score

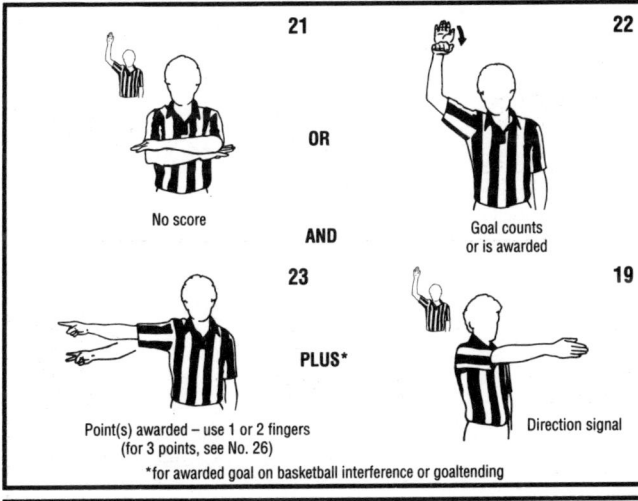

OR

22 Goal counts or is awarded

AND

23 Point(s) awarded – use 1 or 2 fingers
(for 3 points, see No. 26)

PLUS*

19 Direction signal

*for awarded goal on basketball interference or goaltending

25 Visible counts

27 Shot clock violation

28 Shot clock reset

Official Rules 173

Official Signals

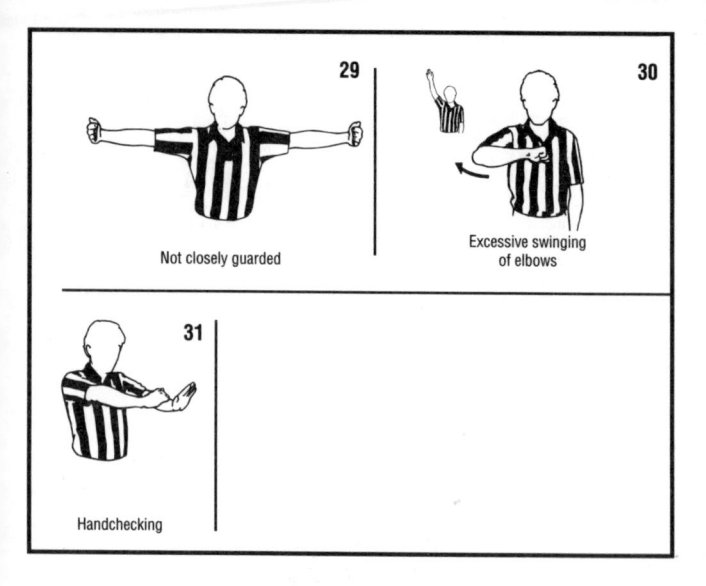

29 Not closely guarded

30 Excessive swinging of elbows

31 Handchecking

Index

Index to Rules

	Rule	Sec.
Alternating process		
center jump	6	2
situations	6	3
Backboards		
see *equipment*		
Backcourt		
definition	4	16
exceptions	9	11
violation	9	11
Ball		
see *equipment*		
Basket		
see *equipment*		
definition	4	1
Basket interference		
definition	4	2
violations/penalties	9	16
Bleeding	5	10
Blocking/charging	4	3
Bonus free throw	4	4
Boundary lines	4	5
Closely guarded	4	6
Control		
alternating-possession process	4	7
definition	4	7
player	4	7
team	4	7
Court/markings		
center circle	1	4
coaching box	1	22
dimensions	1	2

Official Rules

Index to Rules

	Rule	Sec.
division line	1	.5
end lines	1	.3
free-throw lane markings	1	.6
free-throw line markings	1	.7
logos/names	1	.16
restraining lines	1	.3
sidelines	1	.3
three-point field-goal line	1	.23

Dead ball

exceptions	6	.7
situations	6	.7

Disposal of ball

definition	4	.8
free thrower	6	.6

Disqualified player 4 9

Dribble

definition	4	.10
double dribble	9	.6
end of dribble	4	.10
interrupted dribble	4	.10

Dunking .... 4 .... .11
Elastic power 2 4
Electronic transmission 10 5

Equipment

backboards

dimensions	1	.8
logos/names	1	.16
padding	1	.9
position	1	.11
support systems	1	.10

ball

logos/names	1	.14
provided by	1	.17

Index to Rules

	Rule	Sec.
specifications	1	14
baskets		
material	1	12
position	1	13
size	1	12
game-clock display	1	18
logos/names	1	16
players	3	6
possession indicator	1	20
scoreboard	1	18
scorers'/timers' table	1	21
shot-clock display	1	19
team benches	1	21
testing and approval	1	15
Extra period	4	12
Fighting		
definition	4	13
penalty	10	8
Forfeited game		
definition	5	4
scorer	5	4
statistics	5	4
technical foul forfeiture	10	1
Foul		
common	4	14
definition	4	14
disqualified player	4	9
double personal	4	14
double technical	4	14
false double	4	14
flagrant	4	14
intentional	4	14
multiple	4	14

Official Rules   179

Index to Rules

	Rule	Sec.
personal	4	14
player-control	4	14
technical	4	14

Free throw

ball in play		
after false double foul	8	6
if missed	8	5
bonus	4	4
definition	4	15
lane markings	1	6
line markings	1	7
next play	8	4
positions during attempt	8	1
provisions	9	1
ten-second limit	8	3
violation penalties	9	2
by each team	9	2
by free thrower	9	2
by free thrower's team	9	2
by opponent	9	2
who attempts	8	2
personal fouls	8	2
technical fouls	8	2

Front court/backcourt

definition	4	16
violation	9	11

Fumble	4	17

Game

how started	6	1
objective	1	1

Goal	5	1

Goaltending

definition	4	18
situations	9	15

Index to Rules

	Rule	Sec.
violations/penalties	9	16
Guarding		
definition	4	19
legal position	4	19
on person with ball	4	19
on person without ball	4	19
time and distance	4	19
Hands/arms, legal use	4	20
Held ball		
alternating-possession	6	3
definition	4	21
Holding	4	22
Incidental contact	4	23
Interrupted game	5	5
Jump ball		
alternating-possession	6	2
definition	4	24
position for	6	4
violation	9	7
Location of player	4	25
Logos/names		
backboard	1	16
ball	1	14
court	1	16
Multiple throw	4	26
No contest	5	4
Officials		
approval of score	2	3
correctable errors	2	10
elastic power	2	4
jurisdiction	2	8
referee	2	1
duties	2	2

Index to Rules

	Rule	Sec.
scorer's duties	2	11
shot-clock operator's duties	2	13
signals	2	9
fouls	2	9
throw-ins	2	9
television monitors	2	5
timer's duties	2	12
umpires	2	1
when decisions differ	2	7
Out of bounds		
ball	7	1
ball awarded	7	4
ball caused to go out	7	2
ball in play from	7	5
ball touched simultaneously	7	3
player	7	1
violation	9	3
Pass	4	27
Penalty	4	28
Periods		
beginning	5	8
end	5	8
length of	5	7
Personal foul		
by dribbler	10	10
by screener	10	11
penalties	10	12
free throws	10	12
exception	10	12
types	10	9
Pivot	4	29
Protests	5	6
Rule	4	30

Index to Rules

	Rule	**Sec.**

Scoring
- free throw 5 2
- opponent's basket 5 2
- three-point goal .5 2
- two-point goal 5 2

Screen
- definition 4 31
- personal foul 10 9

Shot clock
- display 1 19
- duties of operator 2 13
- violation 9 10

Shot-clock try 4 32

Substitutions
- entry into game .3 4
- technical foul 10 2

Tap 4 33

Team
- captain 3 2
- composition 3 1
- lineup 3 3

Technical foul
- administrative 10 2
    - delay of game 10 2
    - excessive timeouts 10 2
    - musical instruments 10 2
    - number of participants 10 2
    - penalty 10 2
    - starting lineup/squad list . .10 2
    - substitution 10 2
- bench-area restrictions 10 7
    - penalty 10 7
- conduct, players 10 3
    - penalty 10 3

Official Rules

Index to Rules

	Rule	Sec.
fighting	10	8
definition	4	13
penalty	10	8
flagrant	10	6
definition	4	14
penalty	10	6
forfeiture	10	1
unsporting conduct		
bench personnel	10	5
coaches	10	5
followers/fans	10	5
penalty		
bench personnel	10	5
players	10	4
substitutes	10	5
team attendants	10	5
Television monitors	2	5
Television replay equipment	10	5
Ten-second violation	9	9
Three-second violation	9	8
Throw-in		
count	7	6
definition	4	34
resumption of play	6	5
start	7	6
violation	9	4
Tie score	5	9
Timeout		
charged	5	11
excessive	5	13
injury	5	10
length	5	11
number allowed	5	11

Index to Rules

	Rule	Sec.
successive	5	11
starting clocks	5	12
stopping clocks	5	10
technical foul penalty	10	2
20-second	5	11
who requests	5	11

Traveling
definition	4	35
establishing pivot foot	4	35
violation	9	5

Try for field goal
airborne shooter exception	4	36
definition	4	36

Uniforms
commemorative patches	3	5
logos/decals	3	5
names	3	5
numbers	3	5
shirts	3	5
shorts	3	5
specifications	3	5
tights	3	5

Unsporting conduct
foul	4	14
official's penalty	2	6
player's conduct	10	4

Verticality
components	4	37
definition	4	37

Violations/penalties
backcourt	9	11
ball out of bounds	9	3
basket interference	9	15
penalties	9	16

Index to Rules

	Rule	Sec.
closely guarded	9	13
definition	4	38
double dribble	9	6
elbow(s)	9	12
floor penalties	9	14
free-throw penalties	9	2
free-throw provisions	9	1
goaltending	9	15
penalties	9	16
jump ball	9	7
shot clock	9	10
ten-second rule	9	9
three-second rule	9	8
throw-in provisions	9	4
travel, kick, fist	9	5
Winning team	5	3